THE PHENOMENON OF WELSHNESS

or
'How many aircraft carriers
would an independent Wales have?'

The Phenomenon of Welshness

or

'How many aircraft carriers
would an independent Wales have?'

Siôn T. Jobbins

First published in 2011

© Siôn T. Jobbins

© Gwasg Carreg Gwalch 2011

Published with the financial support
of the Welsh Books Council

ISBN: 978-1-84527-311-8

Cover design: Sion Ilar

Published by Gwasg Carreg Gwalch,
12 Iard yr Orsaf, Llanrwst, Wales LL26 0EH
tel: 01492 624031
fax: 01492 641502
email: books@carreg-gwalch.com
website: www.carreg-gwalch.com

I Siwan a'r plant
Elliw Lois, Gwenno Lowri ac Owain Mabon,

ac i'm rhieni, Alun a Catrin,
am fy magu mewn ysbryd o gariad a brawdgarwch.

Contents

Map

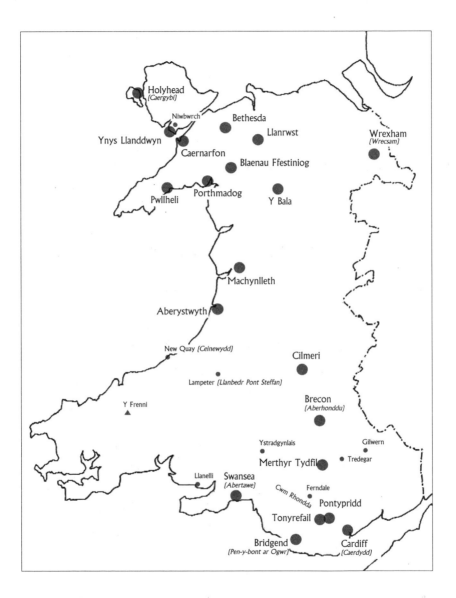

Holyhead
(Caergybi)

Niwbwrch

Bethesda

Llanrwst

Wrexham
[Wrecsam]

Ynys Llanddwyn

Caernarfon

Blaenau Ffestiniog

Pwllheli

Porthmadog

Y Bala

Machynlleth

Aberystwyth

New Quay *(Ceinewydd)*

Cilmeri

Lampeter *(Llanbedr Pont Steffan)*

Y Frenni

Brecon
(Aberhonddu)

Ystradgynlais

Gilwern

Merthyr Tydfil

Tredegar

Llanelli

Swansea
(Abertawe)

Ferndale

Cwm Rhondda

Pontypridd

Tonyrefail

Bridgend
(Pen-y-bont ar Ogwr)

Cardiff
(Caerdydd)

Introduction

Wales since 1960

Imagine, if you will, a person who left Wales in the early 1960s, or one who had not visited the country as a tourist for decades. Or, imagine a person who lives within a few hours of the Welsh border – or, dare I say it, within the Welsh border, but who reads and hears only the news through London. You may know such a person.

There will be many familiar things recalled from the returnee's memory or the occasional news item, which they will recognise as they visit Wales. The rain still falls: Swansea (with around 1360.8 mm per annum in the 1980s) is the wettest city in the UK, after all. The country is still comparatively poorer than the rest of the UK, and even poorer now than some states like Slovenia, which were behind the Iron Curtain. Many of the shops and the banks and even the cafes on the Welsh high streets will be the same as those of Everytown UK: in that respect, all British towns have come to look alike.

But there will also be differences. New buildings and roads: you'd expect that. But probably the most obvious difference will be that road signs have added a language other than English. You'd recognise or maybe remember some words, words like 'pont' for 'bridge', which anyone with school French would know. You'd guess that 'stryd' meant 'street', and after a short while that 'araf' meant 'slow'. Where and when did that happen? You don't remember seeing any articles about that in the press. Even the supermarkets have signs in Welsh and in some, sometimes, tinny announcements in Welsh on the Tannoy too.

As you tune your car radio and try and avoid the ever-present sheep nonchalantly munching the green grass, you'll stumble across pop music. You start tapping your fingers on the steering wheel, trying to mouth the words, until you realise it's not some unknown American or European English song but a different language. Your hotel room will have a television with soccer matches from Spain and Italy with Welsh commentary, or whole programmes and concerts from the Eisteddfod. In so many ways, everything is familiar, and yet it isn't.

What has happened is that Wales has been through a revolution over the past forty-odd years and you probably hadn't heard of it: a revolution which killed no English person and barely made the headlines anywhere across the world; a quiet, barely-noticed revolution, not like the one across the water in Ireland. Not only has Welsh society been revolutionised, but the fabric of that society has been changed utterly too. You may have read articles in the *Guardian* or heard on the BBC about the 'transmigration' of people from Indonesia to West Papua; you'll have heard that Tibetans are in danger of becoming a minority in Tibet to the Han Chinese; but you hadn't realised that so many people had moved from England into Wales. That's one reason you may not hear as much Welsh on the street as during your last visit. Like the Tibetans, many Welsh people feel the melancholy of being internal exiles: strangers in their own land. Why are there features in the media on the same situation in faraway lands, when it exists on your doorstep for the speakers of the original language of this island?

You would probably have heard that Wales had its own Assembly – you're well-read after all. But would you know why there was a change in Welsh society between the devolution 'No' Vote of 1979 and the 'Yes' of 1997? That Yes vote, despite the slim majority, signified (and in many ways hid) a much more fundamental change in Welsh society than the solid 'Yes' vote in Scotland which you know so much more about.

Wales not in the news

For the fact is, Wales is a hidden land. Protests and rallies which draw thousands in Wales don't make the London news, whilst protests of a few dozen in faraway lands do. It's a country which is not quite far enough from England, or dangerous enough, to be exciting, and yet not part of England to impinge on the English radar. Wales is a blind spot. Maybe, because we have our own media within the UK, editors can tick off the 'Wales' slot by saying, 'That'll be covered by Cardiff, no need for London to bother'. Maybe you have to kill people to be noticed by the press, and being well-spoken and polite doesn't hit the headlines – too many sons and daughters of the Welsh Manse, maybe!

Maybe it's because so much of what is interesting in Welsh political and artistic life goes on in Welsh, a language which few speak outside Wales. That whole vibrant debate, therefore, is missed, a debate which, without media attention, gets filtered into Welsh public life through friends and acquaintances and bits of translation. In some respects, Welsh society, or, rather, society in Wales, is almost pre-literate. A minority reads Welsh newspapers or even watches Welsh news, in English or Welsh, so that ideas are disseminated orally, not written, almost by some cultural osmosis between friends and within families. These ideas simply don't get picked up by the press outside.

Wales in this book

These chapters (all of which were first published as articles in *Cambria* magazine) won't answer all your questions about what has happened over the past decades, but will answer many of them. It will, hopefully, open the door on the society and history of a country which many know little about.

Wales is a funny place. Yes, both 'funny ha ha' and 'funny peculiar' as they say. After all, how many countries in the world become a measurement of land? The 'size of Wales' ratio has almost gained standard ISO code validation and is used to measure everything from the depletion of the Amazonian rainforest to a medium-sized farm in the Australian outback. We're only 20,000 square kilometres ('the size of Slovenia', since you ask). We make the 'tiny' Baltic states look overweight. Estonia, at 45,000 square kilometres, is over twice the 'size of Wales', but has the misfortune of being next to the huge Russia, which, as we all know is 853.77 times the 'size of Wales'. You know that the inhabitants of a country think the country is big when they measure distance not in miles nor kilometres but in time. So, Cardiff is two and a half hours from Aberystwyth. Which, in any normal European state, is about 300 miles. But in Wales, it's only 110. The trans-Wales transport infrastructure has never again managed to reach the dizzy heights of the time of the Roman empire, when the north-south Sarn Helen road ran from Aberconwy to Carmarthen.

But there's a great diversity within this little 'patch of land'. Wales is a three-city country – there are quite a few in Europe. Wales is one of the oldest. But don't believe the Welsh propaganda. Our language isn't 'the oldest language in Europe', unless, for some unknown reason, speakers of Latin or Slavic or Germanic-derived languages decided to conduct their lives as mutes until about 500 AD, and suddenly started speaking a language which their parents couldn't understand. However, our language does have a fine pedigree, and had a written tradition before many other European ones. There were more books published in Welsh before 1850 than in Finnish or Serbian.

We like our landscape . . . but then maybe we don't. Maybe many of us see the mountains just as faults of geology which were made to keep us poor. Cambrian mountains, of course, aren't made of Cambrian rock, they're made of words and poetry and history, piled on top of each other, like bits of Scrabble, until over millennia they get crushed and crushed to create great seams of tradition and oral history which you have to quarry to keep the memory of those seams alive lest they are lost and forgotten. For mountains without their Welsh names pronounced and understood are punctured and ugly as piled tyres in a garage forecourt. And a river, whose folk memories have been washed away by the stream, isn't a river, it's wet stuff running through a Potemkin village. That's why we get angry and pull down signs. We won't accept that our morality over this piece of land is worthless.

When you meet us
But when we ask you, 'Where are you from?' don't take it personally. Don't get all ratty and touchy and embarrassingly 'right on'. We're just nosy. We're just translating from Welsh the question which is most important. Jobs come and go. But where you're from is eternal. We're not from 'nowhere'; we're from a town or a village. And, if you're an expat reading this, don't say something soft like, 'Oh, I'm from a town between Cardiff and Swansea.' What kind of a dull answer is that? Say you're from Bridgend . . . go on, say it loud and proud . . . Cos you see, we're not big, so everywhere's important.

And there aren't too many of us either, I mean, the globe is hardly tilting over because the world's population of Welsh people has just shot up. And there are even fewer of us that speak Welsh, so, well, every man and woman counts . . .

Trouble is, see, because there aren't that many of us in Wales (2.9 million) and because many speak this language which had no official status in its own country until 1967 – yeah, many of us were quite peeved with that too – it's difficult for us to integrate people into Welsh-language culture.

So, if we seem defensive, put yourselves, if you're English, in our shoes. How would you feel if England had been conquered by Napoleon in 1815, French was made the only official language, everyone had to speak only French at school, English was seen as an inferior language and then shrunk until it's a minority language, and spoken only in England; and then, hey presto: some thirty million French people land on your doorstep complaining and shrugging their shoulders about the silly 'th' sound in 'this' and 'that'.

We could have been like the Irish, who bombed and killed people and then got invited to 10 Downing Street for a cosy chat and cup of tea with the Prime Minister. But in Wales we decided to dodge the killing bit and go straight for the cup of tea.

Is that where we 'went wrong'?

Now this is an exciting time for Wales. We really are building a new country and we're gradually putting together the ideological building blocks for this new Wales. It's built on old foundations which this book will enlighten you about, a little. But we're also looking for a new design – which I have presumptuously, but thoughtfully, outlined for you here too. Gradually we're working out how our new homeland should look. In an age when people can decide to move and live in a country where they'll pay less tax, or where gay rights are more respected, or where the sun shines 300 days a year, or where they can ski during the winter time, or where they can live by Sharia law, should there not be a little piece of land, let's say 20,000 sq km, where they can choose to live their life through the medium of Welsh? Maybe not in every square kilometre of that land, but in at least part of it, and to various degrees? Is that really such a big ask? Is denying that choice denying a choice not only for Welsh people but for anyone, world-wide, who may wish to have that choice too? In a world of diversity, why not have diversity of states?

The issues and challenges which Wales has faced are increasingly becoming the issues which much of the world will now have to face over the coming century; issues of language transmission for minority languages competing with Spanish, Chinese or English; issues of accommodating huge demographic change. Issues of dealing with new information technology, and issues of cultural and political powerlessness.

Wales can lead by example and provide a model for other countries to follow, or avoid. Indeed, the twenty-first century could be the 'Welsh century' for many of the world's people. And that's one of the enriching things about Welsh identity: it offers to the world a live, three-dimensional experience in place of a flat, two-dimensional map.

I'll tell you something. During the 1980s other young people had nightmares about the imminent nuclear Armageddon. Me? In my nightmares the language I spoke would die before I got old, and I'd be left among a handful of sad and lonely people speaking Welsh, this walking-dead language. I won't say everything's sorted, it's not, but I don't have that nightmare any more. And the reason is that there's been a big, big change in Wales. This book will help explain what happened here in the past – and what could happen here in the future.

All these pieces were written for *Cambria* magazine early in the twenty-first century, and have been adapted for this book. I'm indebted to the founder-editor of *Cambria*, Henry Jones-Davies, and his wife (and present editor) Frances, for their support and guidance over the years, and for embarking on creating such an important and lively magazine.

I'd also like to thank Dr Gareth Popkins for casting a kind but critical eye on my articles over the years.

Siôn T. Jobbins
Aberystwyth, December 2010

Hidden Histories

The 1847 Government Report into Education in Wales, which was published in volumes with blue covers (the infamous Blue Books), was to the Welsh-speaking community what the Suez crisis was to the British establishment almost a century later – a deadly knock to confidence and prestige.

From being a nation of rebellious hearts and healthy dreams in the first half of the century, the Blue Books, perhaps more than anything else, made Wales a nation apologetic for being 'too Welsh'. Within a generation, Michael D. Jones set up a Welsh-speaking colony in Patagonia, far away from the malignant effect of the Blue Books. In 1856 James James of Pontypridd, the author of 'Mae hen wlad fy nhadau', the song which would be adopted as our national anthem, instilled a message of defiance in the last line of the chorus, 'O bydded i'r heniaith barhau' ('Oh long may the old language survive'), no doubt in defensive reaction to the new anti-Welsh orthodoxy.

The effects of the Blue Books are still felt today. No understanding of modern Wales is complete without recognition of the mentality that published the report – or, indeed, the mentality of the Welsh people that internalised the colonialising attitude of the report.

It is time our historians and academics studied Welsh history from the perspective of the colonising experience that we've endured – and, some say, are still enduring today.

The legacy of The Blue Books lives on

Two serendipitous events on two different screens opened my eyes one dark winter night. The first was reading pages on a website. It's not often that I study websites and I was left with my jaw dangling like some idiot anthropomorphic dog in a cartoon. There I was reading about debauchery and loose morals, but there wasn't a scantily-clad girl to be seen.

These were the dusty pages of the 1847 Government Report on the State of Education in Wales.

This infamous Report is now online on the National Library of Wales's Digital Mirror pages. It is more commonly known in Welsh as '*Brad y Llyfrau Gleision*' (The Treachery of the Blue Books) – blue because of the colour of the Report's cover. Although I'd always been aware of the Blue Books in the wallpaper of Welsh history, I'd never actually read them or knew anything about them in great detail. The site was a gobsmacker. Listen to this – and these are just from the section covering the counties of Cardiganshire and Powys:

Teach English and bigotry will be banished.
Rev. Denning of St Mary's, Brecon

The Welsh language is a vast drawback to the Welsh and a manifold barrier to the moral progress and commercial prosperity of the people. It is not easy to over-estimate its evil effect.
One of the Report's authors

The Commissioner Henry Penry said of a boy in rural Brecon, that there 'was scarcely any difference between him and a rude or rustic Hottentot'. Children, the Commissioners noted, recited lessons in 'a Welsh screech' and used languages 'for which a beast's cry would do as well'.

Another quote by an interviewee said pompously, 'From my experience of Ireland I think there is a great similarity between the lower orders of the Welsh and Irish – both are dirty, indolent, bigoted and contented.'

One of the biggest concerns of the Report and of members of the establishment who were interviewed was the 'deceiving' influence of the Welsh language especially in courts of law (where, since the acts of incorporation in 1536,

English was the only official language). Credibility was given to the view of a Cardigan barrister, E. C.Hall, that 'the Welsh language is peculiarly evasive, which originates from its having been the language of slavery'.

And it wasn't just the English who were prejudiced against the Welsh language. With friends like the awful Mr Williams, a Lampeter clerk, giving his views on the 'deceiving nature' of the Welsh language in court, who needed enemies? 'There is no remedy for this state of things except the propagation of the English language', he went on.

If the Welsh hadn't taken this condemnation to heart these remarks might even be construed as funny.

From the outset the Report was a colonial weapon aimed at the Welsh-speaking working class. Its remit said quite clearly that it was to look 'especially into the means afforded to the labouring classes of acquiring a knowledge of the English language'. Such a Report, so damning of Welsh morals and of the Welsh language, might have been the catalyst for a mass emancipation movement for Welsh rights. That's what happened in Flanders, where Dutch-speakers faced similar bigotry from the French-speaking establishment as the Francophones strove to make Belgium a French-speaking nation. As in Wales, the languages of the masses came up against the policy and language of the state. In exactly the same year, 1847, in Flanders, a pamphlet published by Henrick Conscience and F. A. Snellaert attacked the 'state of humiliation', and proposed a twelve-point manifesto which included Dutch instruction in all universities and secondary schools, and the use of Dutch in law courts and for technical handbooks, to 'contribute to the cultural and industrial education of the Flemish people'.

Gwyneth Tyson Roberts in her excellent book *The Language of the Blue Books: the perfect instrument of Empire* (University of Wales Press, 1998) draws the correlation between the Government's Report, with its attitude towards the Welsh language, and the governmental attitude to other colonial languages and peoples. 'For Wales, see India',[1] so to speak. Tyson Roberts, a former English lecturer at Baghdad University, refers to the influence of such people as T. B. (later Lord) Macaulay, who drafted a paper in 1835 setting out the argument for making English the sole language of education in the sub-continent, even above such established literary languages as Arabic, Sanskrit, Bengali or Tamil. The nature of questioning of interviewees for the Blue Books mirrors that of a government report on 'Negro' education in the Windward and Leeward Isles of the West Indies. And as Tyson Roberts notes, the attitude and words employed in the reports are very much in the style of James Mills, who believed, astoundingly, that his lack of first-hand knowledge of India and Indian languages could only be an 'advantage in writing an impartial and true history of the country'.

'The success of a policy like Macaulay's,' says Tyson Roberts:

depends precisely upon the creation of this sense of their own inferiority in the colonized people, who, in order that the power of the colonizer can be maintained, must be convinced that all legitimate authority (cultural, social and linguistic as well as political, economic and military) comes from the colonizing power, which alone has the ability to judge rightly themselves, their society and the world in general . . . and official English attitudes to minority languages within Britain used the same theories to assert and justify the right of English to be regarded as the only valid language of Britain.

---

[1] In the first edition of *Encyclopaedia Britannica* the entry for Wales famously read 'For Wales, see "England"'.

As we saw in 2001 with the furore in the *Welsh Mirror* and on the floor of the Assembly over the Seimon Glyn affair (see 'Beyond the Pale' later in this book) – arguments for social and economic progress are still being used to undermine the Welsh language. These same arguments were used to undermine other native languages in India and Africa. The Blue Books were clearly, therefore, a colonial tool. Gwyneth Tyson Roberts says in the introduction to her book that:

> any measure which induced the Welsh to forget their own language, and to learn and operate entirely through English, thus had considerable advantages for the equilibrium of the British state; it would not only facilitate communication but would assert official (English) authority over the Welsh people.

And the Blue Books have been astonishingly successful in their centralising remit, for they have created a current Wales in which a person can be a Welshman and not speak Welsh, but can't be a Welshman and not speak English. The Report's success, of which Macaulay would be proud, was to create a Welsh identity which for a large part of our population is mostly a cultural identity within a greater, more powerful civic English identity – the 'true legitimate authority'. For many, and even some who support the call for more powers to the Assembly, this civic English/Welsh identity means a Wales just like Guernsey or Jersey rather than a real nation. A state with an Assembly but an Assembly without a nation.

In light of the transparently colonial nature of the Blue Books and other deliberately colonial policies towards Wales and her language, the weakness – nay, the very invisibility – of a colonial historiography of Welsh history is all the more surprising. Among the religious, feminist, left-wing or touristic historiographies, to name but a few, a colonial historiography is absent. I could not find a single one of the 15,000 theses presented to the University of Wales since 1988 which gives a colonial interpretation of Welsh history. This despite papers submitted on 'colonial education in Sint Maarten' (a Dutch Caribbean island) and a few on the colonisation of North America and Australia.

Is a colonial interpretation of Welsh history the historiography which 'dare not speak its name' in the corridors of Welsh academia? Would a lecturer see his future blackballed were he or she to present a module of Welsh history as the history of a deliberately colonised nation?

Or is the fault deeper than that? Has the Blue Books syndrome seeped so deep into our psyche that we will not even admit to having been colonised – almost like someone unable to admit to having been raped? Is it too difficult for us to mention our colonisation, lest it hurt, or to question our interviewing boards, our television commissioners, our Assembly Members?

Has the National Movement itself been so enfeebled that even it can't speak the word 'colonisation' where Wales is concerned – but can for nations overseas? Is not our nationalist historiography in itself the historiography of the defeated, which is beautifully and subconsciously evoked by Dafydd Iwan's iconic song, ''Yma o Hyd'!' (still here!). Yes, 'Yma o Hyd', not so much a defiant call to arms but a stoical shrug of the shoulders – the resigned fatalism of the loser? 'Yma o Hyd'! – hey it's not that bad, boys, look, we're not as bad off as the Bretons, we're still here – just about. A historiography which is but lists of those which have done their best for (in the words of the late George Thomas, an anti-devolutionist) 'little old Wales', but is not a coherent school of thought.

But in my week of goggle-eyed Blue Book reading in 2005, a programme serendipitously leapt to life on S4C:

Popeth yn Gymraeg. A six-part series broadcast every evening at 9.00 on the bridge of November and December. A series which sent keyboards tapping on the Welsh-language blogs and the discussion forum, maes-e.com, the forum which Simon Brooks, editor of *Barn*, called 'the Welsh street'. One contributor on maes-e asked if this was the most important broadcast on the Welsh media since Saunders Lewis's famous 1962 *Tynged yr Iaith* (the fate of the language) lecture, in which Saunders correctly said 'through revolutionary means only can we succeed'.

Popeth yn Gymraeg (everything in Welsh) was simple but immense. Ifor ap Glyn, a London Welshman who is now a television producer and a cliché-free poet, visited the four corners of Wales speaking Welsh, yes, and only Welsh. To everyone. As he said on the website which accompanied the series (and which should still be available to read if only S4C had an 'archive' setting on its site) he switched off the linguistic 'radar' which all Welsh-speakers have: that is the radar programmed into every Welsh-speaker to judge a person by their clothes, looks, confidence, locality, age and a myriad of other prejudices to sum up in a nanosecond if the person siarads Cymraeg or not. Ap Glyn treated everyone equally. Everyone can or could speak Welsh, and if they didn't he wasn't going to apologise and switch to English but rather continue politely, and with grace and good humour, to speak to them in Welsh.

This, in a colonised country like Wales, is revolutionary stuff – you had only to see the look of utter nervousness and dread on the faces of half a dozen people who'd agreed to follow Ifor ap Glyn's example in the dangerous streets and shops of Aberystwyth, to realise that. How revolutionary? Well consider this. A man walks into the Cabin Café in Aberystwyth. Not any man, but a professor at the university. A man who, by the general norms of society, every society, was in a 'position of superiority' over the young girl serving in the café. By virtue of his profession, age, wage, sex, cut-of-his-cloth, status in society, and also – in a capitalist country – being a customer, he would generally be considered to have the 'upper hand' in the situation. Yet this man didn't have the confidence to ask the young girl behind the counter for a simple 'paned o goffi, plîs' in case she spoke no Welsh. And this man was a lecturer in the Welsh Department! No matter how 'low' the job esteem is, its esteem can never be lower than the Welsh language. Heavens, you could walk into any café in Europe and ask in Welsh for a 'paned o goffi, plîs' and they'd figure out you weren't asking for a bag of turnips!

Politicians who speak the language of glib should try speaking Welsh in shops and pubs across Wales and see what it is to feel a foreigner in your own country. Thanks, in part, to the Blue Books, most Welsh-speakers have given up, have accepted colonisation, and saved themselves the embarrassment and hassle.

But should speaking Welsh and not switching to English be so difficult? In theory, everyone under the age of twenty-five has had years of Welsh lessons and should know some basic Welsh. As Ifor ap Glyn found out, many people who said they spoke no Welsh actually had quite a lot stored 'up there', more than they realised, and were quite willing to give it a go. When Eliezer ben Yehuda, the man who revived the 'dead' Hebrew language disembarked from his ship in Jaffa in 1881 and decided he would speak only Hebrew, the people, like in Wales, weren't totally devoid of the language. Every Jewish man had a rudimentary understanding of the language through Biblical studies at the synagogue; the same is true in a different context in Wales. Knowledge wasn't the problem, it was *attitude*. So, Eliezer son of Yehuda travelled to Jerusalem as Ifor son of Glyn travelled to Aberystwyth, Wrexham and Blaenau Gwent.

The 21 per cent who, according to the 2001 census, speak Welsh, is greater than the number who spoke fluent Hebrew in ben Yehuda's time, and about the same percentage as those fluent *English* speakers in Wales at the time of the Blue Books. Yes, languages are about information and communication, but what the three authors of the Blue Books and Ifor ap Glyn realised is that languages are about power too. They're also about morality – the immorality of the subjection and colonisation of the Welsh language and the morality of reviving it.

Cambria, volume 7, number 6, January–February 2006

It was at the funeral of the Rev Ifan Williams that the little-known story of Ysgol Glyndŵr was re-awoken in me. Ifan was a supporter of the school; his daughters Elin and Siwan had attended it.

The founders of the school, Trefor and Gwyneth Morgan, were brave and imaginative people who were attacked on both sides for their venture. As so often in history, it was only in hindsight that many people could appreciate their contribution and cultural entrepreneurship. Unfortunately, that was only after Trefor and Gwyneth had been through some personal hardship and deliberate misunderstanding from those opposed to Welsh-medium education, and from supporters of Welsh-medium education who tried to over-compensate their left-wing credentials by also attacking the school for being 'elitist'.

Writing an article over forty years later about a couple I never knew was a little worrying. It was very gratifying for me, then, after the article was published in Cambria magazine, to receive a letter from Branwen Jarvis, Trefor and Gwyneth's daughter, saying that I'd succeeded in getting their story across. Forty-one years later, Leighton Andrews AM announced the first-ever, and very long-awaited education strategy for the Welsh language.

Glyndŵr's school

Were someone to tell you that a private Welsh-medium school was founded in 1968, would you bracket it conveniently with the famous 'posh' schools of England? Or would you place it as an effort by concerned families to answer a need which local authorities had failed (or refused) to undertake?

That's the question which was raised back in 1968 when Ysgol Glyndŵr was opened in Bridgend – the culmination of the zeal and finance of the charismatic Trefor Morgan, a small man with a burning love of Wales and her language.

He was born in 1914 in Tonyrefail, the fifth child of a stonemason who died in the great flu pandemic of 1918. Although Trefor won a place at the local grammar school his family's poverty forced him to work at the local coal mine, despite his poor health. He became one of the early nationalists and was a conscientious objector during the War. He stood for Plaid Cymru during the 1940s and 1950s, losing to many MPs whose names and legacies have long been forgotten. But Morgan was a born entrepreneur. He established Undeb, an insurance and finance company in Aberdare, and succeeded in establishing a small trading estate. The profits from Undeb were to be used for two purposes: establishing small local industries – and promoting the creation of Welsh-medium schools throughout Wales.

He founded Cronfa Glyndŵr yr Ysgolion Cymreig (the Glyndŵr Fund for Welsh-medium Schools) in 1963. The most important aspect was creating and maintaining Welsh-medium nursery schools, but because of the reluctance of local authorities to offer secondary school education in Welsh he founded Ysgol Glyndŵr in 1968.

The school was opened at Bryntirion, Laleston, near Bridgend, on the site of an old private school and what is now an Evangelical Christian Centre. It was both a junior and a high school. Although Ysgol Gyfun Rhydfelen in nearby Pontypridd had opened in 1962, Trefor Morgan and others felt the school didn't show enough confidence in, or respect for, the Welsh language, as many subjects were still taught in English. Ysgol Glyndŵr would be different. It would be the first totally Welsh-medium school. Like the Hebrew renaissance in Israel, there would be no subject which could not be taught through the Welsh language, including mathematics and the sciences.

Elin Hefin was one of the pupils at the high school part of Ysgol Glyndŵr. Her father, the late Rev. Ifan Williams, a Baptist minister in Bridgend, was forced to resign his chapel because the denomination disagreed with his support for Cymdeithas yr Iaith and the Welsh language. He was a friend of Trefor Morgan and lived opposite the school. Elin and her sister Siwan were two of only six children in the new comprehensive side of the school. Elin still remembers the grey socks and grey and light blue '*brethyn*' (Welsh tweed) school uniform tunics, the school badge with a Celtic cross, and the rather cryptic motto '*gan brynu'r amser*' ('by buying time'). Most of all she remembers the school for its 'amazing' teachers: Elin Garlick, Jack Harries, Rita Bohana and Falmai Pugh. Another teacher was the young Gerallt Llwyd Owen, who would win the Urdd Chair in 1969, the year of the investiture of Charles Windsor as Prince of Wales, for his cycle of poems which included the now famous verse about Llywelyn, the last native prince of Wales:

> Wylit, wylit Lywelyn,
> wylit waed pe gwelyt hyn.
> Ein calon gan dramorwr,
> ein coron gan estron ŵr.
>
> *(You would weep, weep, Llywelyn,*
> *you would weep blood to see this.*
> *Our heart with a foreign man,*
> *our crown with a conqueror.)*

This radical poem was written in his dormitory in Ysgol Glyndŵr. It caused a split among the Eisteddfod audience, and was booed by the establishment, but roared at with approval by the mostly younger audience when Dafydd Iwan read the poem at the Noson Lawen event at the Urdd Eisteddfod that year.

Another teacher was Gwyneth Morgan, Trefor's wife. Where Trefor was the heavy-smoking sometime pool-hustling entrepreneur, proud to drive his Jaguar car, Gwyneth could be a strict but effective driving force in her own right.

The school was fee-paying, and as one can well imagine this created some disquiet among both supporters and opponents of Welsh-medium education.

Some who were pro-Welsh-medium education believed that the county council and state should finance Welsh education in the same way that it financed English-medium education. There was a moral question here and they were uneasy that the new school was 'giving in' by opting out. There was also a niggling concern at seeing the Welsh language equated with such un-socialist and 'un-Welsh' concepts as fee-paying education. The fact that the Welsh word for private school is 'ysgol fonedd' (gentry school) only makes any debate on the issue even more difficult. Some class warrior opponents of Welsh-medium education, of course, were ready enough to make that equation, an equation which is still heard from time to time even today, that Welsh schools are 'middle class' or for 'snobs'.

Elitism couldn't be further from Trefor and Gwyneth Morgan's mind. Bryan James, who first met Trefor as a young teacher in Ynysgedwyn, Ystradgynlais, got to know both of them well and is now Secretary of Cronfa Glyndŵr. Speaking in Welsh he recalled:

> There was nothing further from their mind than the concept of a 'gentry school'. They were republicans and at the time this was the only way of offering a wholly Welsh-medium education anywhere in the country ...

they would give of their own money to support any parent who shared the same vision as theirs but couldn't afford the cost.

In this respect, one should view Ysgol Glyndŵr more in the context of the Breton-medium *Diwan* schools. These schools are also fee-paying, but only because the French state refuses to fund Breton-medium schools in the same way that it funds French-medium ones.

Trefor and Gwyneth Morgan had great plans for the school, among many things believing it could develop to be a boarding school and so offer Welsh-medium education to children whose parents lived further afield. Unfortunately, their dreams were cut short by the untimely death of Trefor in 1970 at the age of just fifty-five. Pupils like Elin Hefin then returned to attend Rhydfelen or Ystalyfera, the only two bilingual schools in the whole of Glamorgan. (Bilingual schools have English-medium and Welsh-medium streams.)

Was Trefor Morgan's an impossible dream, like that of another great nationalist, the economist D. J. Davies, with his Danish-style 'folk school' at Pantybeiliau mansion in Gilwern, Gwent? Was it ahead of its time? It could be argued that the slow but gradual rise in bilingual and Welsh-medium education would have continued without Ysgol Glyndŵr, but I tend to believe that it moved things up a gear and is an echo of another school opening thirty years earlier.

September 1939 will be remembered for Hitler's troops marching into Poland. But we in Wales also have a happier anniversary which we should not forget. For in that month seven small children attended Ysgol Gymraeg yr Urdd on Llanbadarn Road at Aberystwyth, a fee-paying school, which opened at the headquarters of the Urdd (the Welsh-speaking youth movement), now sadly demolished with no plaque to record its existence. Like all historic developments in Welsh-medium education, it took place on the linguistic border where Welsh was losing ground. Like Ysgol Glyndŵr, it took one person to become the driving force, in this case Sir Ifan ab Owain Edwards, the founder of the Urdd. The school didn't stay fee-paying for long and soon came under the umbrella of the local authority.

The establishment of Ysgol Glyndŵr mirrors that of the Ysgol Gymraeg in Aberystwyth. It showed what was possible and questioned the principles and morality of politicians and authorities. As Bryan James notes, in the area served by Ysgol Glyndŵr there are now eighteen Welsh-medium high schools, including a new one, Ysgol Gyfun Gymraeg Llangynwyd, in Maesteg, near Bridgend.

But let's not become too smug in our success of Welsh-medium education. A closer reading of the facts show there's no room for complacency – a look at the numbers who take Welsh as first language GCSE is a more honest picture than much of the spin. Assembly Ministers and strategists still confuse Welsh-medium and bilingual schools. As Trefor Morgan and other pioneers knew too well, in the anglicised parts of Wales – and let's face it, all parts of Wales are today anglicised – only Welsh-medium's track-record produces pupils, from whichever ethnic and linguistic background, who are fluent in both Welsh and English. So-called 'bilingual' schools very often do little more than confirm the ethno-linguistic background of the child, and don't assimilate children from non-Welsh-speaking backgrounds – which, of course, is one reason many politicians might prefer these over Welsh-medium schools. Trefor Morgan's battle still isn't wholly won.

Trefor's death wasn't the end of his legacy. A house at the Welsh-language and heritage centre in Nant Gwrtheyrn on the Llŷn peninsular was renovated with his money and named 'Treforgan'. Cronfa Glyndŵr is also still awarding grants to parents and organisations or schools to facilitate

Welsh-medium education, and is currently involved with debate about Welsh-medium education in Carmarthenshire. Maybe his dream of a Welsh-medium boarding school may not have been so far-fetched either. As Wales develops an indigenous ruling class who may often be out of the country or working long hours, will they inevitably look for a Welsh-language boarding school? What of 150,000 Welsh-speakers living in other parts of the UK, many still drawn to London? Is there a market yet for a boarding school which equips children with fully bilingual skills – skills which are increasingly in demand?

Reading about the history of Ysgol Glyndŵr I am struck by the atmosphere of bravery, optimism and 'can do' of the 1960s. Maybe we've lost some of that. We're right to insist that the state should take steps to cater for and plan to 'grow' the Welsh language in Wales, as it did for the English language in Wales. But out of adversity there is also comradeship and strength. The Basques have their *Korrika* and Bretons *Redadeg*, for instance – massive 24-hour relay races across their land with parents, kids and supporters raising money for their schools and education in their own languages. By their efforts, and the efforts of people such as Trefor and Gwyneth Morgan, stronger individuals and stronger communities are created.

Like Glyndŵr himself, Trefor and Gwyneth Morgan's dream hasn't died.

Cambria, volume 11, number 2, July–August 2009

I remember as a young teenager in the early 1980s going with Crwys Road Sunday School in Cardiff up to the Rhondda Valley for a concert of some sort. I don't remember where it was or quite the nature of the event, but it stuck with me as it was such a rare occasion. Sitting on those hard benches, bored at the proceedings, I also felt that I'd been transported back to a time before I was born.

Somewhere in the folk memory of my upbringing I must have been made aware of the '04 Revival (maybe it was the Evan Roberts tea set in my parents' dresser). And as I sat in this three-sizes-too-big chapel that smelt of wood polish and dampness I thought to myself: this was the kind of place that was the beating, thumping heart of the Revival.

A century after the great event I still have mixed emotions. Who can read the reports of the revival, published almost daily in the Western Mail, *and not feel the great excitement it must have generated? And yet, what do we have to show for it? The Theological College opened in Aberystwyth in its wake, but was forced to close a century after it was opened. Was it the wrong revival at the wrong time?*

Remembering the '04

The year 2004 marked the centenary of the last great religious revival in Wales, known colloquially as 'the Evan Roberts Revival'. Television programmes were produced, such as 'A History of Welsh Religion' presented by Huw Edwards; exhibitions (including one at the National Library of Wales); videos, books, and there was even a musical under the guidance of Mal Pope . . . it's what you might call 'a revival of the Revival'.

The Revival began in New Quay, Ceredigion, in February 1904, when a young woman, Florrie Evans, stood up in chapel and declared that she loved God with all her heart. But it was Evan Roberts, a 26-year-old collier at Loughor, near Swansea, who was also a theological student, whom we associate with the great events. Over little more than twelve months Roberts made three great preaching tours: across the southern coalfields, the northern counties, and into Liverpool. Pubs closed, people stopped playing sports and gambling. Colliers who made up a quarter of the Welsh workforce at the time would come off their hard, grimy shift and go straight to a prayer meeting. The chapels were full and the hymn '*I Achub Hen Rebel fel Fi*' ('to save an old rebel like me'), still popular today, came to be associated with the great resurgence. The *Western Mail*, with a closer eye on profit sheet than on hymn sheet, brought out regular supplements costing a shilling and chronicling the Revival's latest events. When I read these pamphlets, with their match-score tally of converts, I sense the exciting, invigorating experience of the Revival and something of the vibrancy of Welsh life a century ago. Amidst the hardship and poverty, places like Maesteg and Ystalafera were young, throbbing centres of work, confidence and debate, brimming with people. What a contrast with the sad, forgotten places they are today!

1904 still plays a big part in the collective memory of the nation. It says much about Welsh history that our only apostrophised date is 'The '04' – a religious revival – whereas the Irish have a series of heroic battles, 'The '98' and 'The '16', and the Scots have 'The '45'.

It's not surprising that in the popular historiography of Wales (especially of Welsh-speaking Wales), Christianity, especially Nonconformism, is seen as a Good Thing. It is credited with saving the language, as well as souls, and you can't get much better than that! Wales' Christian credentials are worn, a proud and honest identity amongst the nations of the world. But how much was Nonconformity, and yes, revivals like the '04, part of our *problem* as a nation, rather than a solution? The answer, of course, partly depends if you are 'of faith' or not, but let's take a look from the perspective of Wales as a nation, and of its language.

There is no doubting the instrumental part religion played in 'saving' the Welsh tongue. In 1549 Elizabeth I decreed that English was to be the sole language of religious services in her Kingdom. The Cornish rebelled and were defeated. By 1563 Elizabeth had softened a little, possibly because of canvassing by Welsh members of her Tudor court. In a shrewd move to consolidate her Realm (and in the one lucky fluke in Welsh history) the Queen decreed that there was to be a Bible in Welsh by 1567. The intention, it seems, was to place the Welsh and English Bible side by side so that the Welsh would learn English more quickly. The Welsh Bible was translated by William Morgan. He worked not from the English but from the original Hebrew and Greek. His Bible was finally published in 1588. It was one of the first complete Bibles in any non-state language, and it fixed and popularised the standard literary language. (Coincidentally, as well as being the centenary of the '04, 2004 was also the 400th anniversary of the death of William Morgan.)

Although Elizabeth I had intended this to strengthen her new Anglican Church, established religion never effectively replaced the old Catholic faith in Wales. Instead, from the eighteenth century onwards there were periodic established revivals, which threw up new leaders and a new counter-culture. Nonconformist denominations, less state-bound and pedestrian than the Anglican church, tapped into the frustration and aspirations of the Welsh-speaking masses, giving solace, strength and status to the people in their own language. The various Nonconformist sects became the dominant religion and culture of the Welsh. In a less aggressive and violent mirror image of the Irish and

Catholicism, to be Welsh was to be Nonconformist. Maybe that's where the problem lies. Maybe, Welsh Nonconformity fatally hindered the development of the Welsh language and a strident Welsh political identity.

In the crucial mid nineteenth-century period when other stateless nations experienced the growth of their new national consciousnesses, the strength of the denominational press in Wales was one of the contributing factors to the failure to create a daily newspaper in Welsh, despite the calls of such as R. J. Derfel, and despite what happened with other smaller nations, like the Estonians and Latvians establishing daily newspapers in their own languages. Nonconformism created a ghettoised Welsh counter-culture, with its own institutions and networks. Much like the mosque in modern Britain, it gave status and a network of advancement for members of the minority ethnic group, which the civic identity of the state denied.

Throughout the 'long nineteenth century' the British state squeezed the Welsh language out of Wales through the law courts, the new institutions of the county councils, and the notorious 'Welsh Not' of the 1870 Education Act. Welsh Nonconformism was a Welsh-speaking refuge and succour. Religion became more than faith. It became an ethnic badge, just as Islam is for many immigrants to Europe today. In the *Report on Religion in England and Wales: findings from the 2001 Home Office Citizenship Survey,* when asked to name the top ten things that would say something important about the respondent, whites, blacks and Asians answered 'family' first of all. However, whereas whites rated 'religion' as tenth in the list, blacks stated 'religion' in third place and Asians put it up in second place. Many Europeans are afraid of Muslims because of the muscular political nature of their religion. Religion in Victorian and Edwardian Wales, in contrast, was the safe, inoffensive music-hall-Welshness that the British state was happy to allow.

The campaign for the disestablishment of the Church sapped generations of Welsh political leaders. They, and the anti-alcohol campaigns, were the only Welsh political results of religious difference. There was no mass language campaign: Welsh Nonconformism was a pliant accomplice in the slow death of the Welsh language, not its saviour.

To read the Welsh press of the nineteenth century is to be struck with the importance of religion in Welsh life. This was the one subject that exercised Welsh minds and milked the country's intellectual energy, much to the detriment of our language and national development. Rather than saving the language, the Sunday school, however successful, acted as an educational ghetto, diverting energy from campaigning against the Welsh Not.[2] For as long as Nonconformism was the badge of Welsh identity, the British state could continue its strategy of creating compliant Welsh subjects. The Revival of 1904 was a shot in the arm for a religious cultural movement, which intellectually stonewalled the development of a civic, assertive Welsh-speaking identity. 1904 prolonged the frigid long Victorian age that did so much to weaken the Welsh language.

It could all have been so different. In 1905, Slovenia didn't have a Revival. Instead, the Slovene national movement almost brought down the autocratic Tisza government of Hungary because of Tisza's refusal to educate Slovenes in Slovene. There was no religious revival in the equally Catholic Basque Country either: instead, also in 1905, Sabin Aran founded the Partido Nacional Vasco, the

---

[2] The 'Welsh Not' was a punitive strategy employed within schools in the nineteenth and early twentieth century. It was a plank with 'Welsh Not' written on it, hanging from a rope, and it was hung around a child's neck if he had been heard speaking Welsh. The child had to pass it on to any other child speaking Welsh; the last one wearing it at the end of the day got the cane. Similar tactics were used to discourage the speaking of Breton in Brittany or Occitane in France.

Basque nationalist party. As a result, the Basque National Movement gained twenty vital years on the Welsh.

In his study of the development of national movements in stateless nations, the Czech historian Miroslav Hroch pinpoints the importance of the contribution of indigenous community leaders, such as ministers and schoolteachers. Many leading figures in Welsh national life came from this Nonconformist background. They could have led the campaign for rights for the Welsh language, which their peers in other small stateless nations (such as Estonia and the Czech lands) did in the nineteenth century. They failed to do so. In fact, the Nonconformists were a very conformist lot.

In a cross-cultural and European perspective, the advancement of Welsh came from Anglicans like Thomas Price (Carnhuanawc), the vicar of Llanfihangel Cwmdu in Brecknockshire, who, as a man before his time, advocated Welsh-medium education in the early nineteenth century; Griffith Jones, Llanddowror, whose 'hedge-schools' taught possibly half the Welsh population of the time to read and write Welsh, was an Anglican, not a Nonconformist. And in the twentieth century, it fell to the dramatist, novelist and language campaigner Saunders Lewis, who had converted from Methodism to Catholicism to open up new possibilities for the Welsh language.

Our Nonconformist ministers and believers did start taking Welsh language and constitutional identity seriously, but only after the rude awakening of the First World War. By then it was very much too late. In fact, linguistic rights for the Welsh language and the development of a radical constitutional agenda in Wales are in inverse proportion to the strength of Nonconformist religion in the country: the more Wales turned away from Nonconformism, the stronger have become the calls for status for the Welsh language and national aspirations. So much for Nonconformism being a badge of Welsh-language identity.

Nonconformism has created a psychiatrist's couch full of complexes for the Welsh. One of the most pernicious complexes is the urge to justify Welshness. This harks back to the concept of Wales being *'gwlad y menyg gwynion'* (the country of the white gloves), which developed in the Victorian age. This racism of the defeated, which held that Wales was cleaner and purer than anywhere else (i.e. England), supposed that God or a government minister could sweep his fingers across Wales without dirtying his white gloves. Just being Welsh wasn't good enough, or radical enough. The country had to be extra-Christian as well. Today, Wales on Wales's own terms has to be more left-wing than England to justify its existence.

Welsh Nonconformism created a nation which was Protestant but without the Protestant work ethic, middle-class without being confident, bourgeois without being mercantile. It left a nation respectable but ridiculed, with a Welsh language that was ethnic, not civic.

We spent the nineteenth century on our knees in our chapels, but for what? It's right that we remember and celebrate Evan Roberts, and the Revival of 1904, but it's worth remembering the consequences of that revival. Maybe it would have been better if Evan Roberts hadn't saved old rebels but had left them to rebel. It would have been better if the Welsh had muscled in on the grubby work of putting their language and culture in their rightful place on their imperfect Earth – whether or not that gained us the approval of our neighbours to the east or west.

Cambria, volume 6, number 5, September–October 2004

I've always wanted to travel back in time to witness the exact birth of an idea which becomes a historic reality: not so much the big famous events like the Gavrilo Princip shooting of Archduke Ferdinand in July 1914, but the first meeting between Princip and his fellow Black Hand conspirators; and not just big political events, either, but happier and quietly-spoken events, like the time Prince Albert planted the first Christmas tree in Buckingham Palace.

With this in mind, I tried to find the conception of St Dwynwen's Day, the day for Welsh lovers. How is a tradition invented? Who invents it? And why? And why is one invented tradition successful and another not? Writing for Cambria magazine gives me the excuse to become a cultural detective and, in doing so, learn so much about my own country. Although I had known of Jane Edwards for years, I never knew that she was the initial 'brains' behind Dwynwen.

It was also gratifying, after publication, to receive a word of thanks from Jane, 'the woman in the mini skirt'.

St Dwynwen's Day

'Welsh romance' may sound like an oxymoron to some, but every year thousands of hopeful singles and smug couples celebrate our patron saint of love on 25 January, St Dwynwen's Day.

Dwynwen was one of the twenty-four daughters of Brychan Brycheiniog, the sixth-century king of southern Wales. Dwynwen's love for Maelon against her father's will led to an unhappy ending, with Dwynwen asking for three wishes including never to remarry, and to be the patron saint of love. The church at Ynys Llanddwyn on Anglesey is dedicated to her and has been a place of pilgrimage for over a millennium.

But although the Dwynwen story is fifty generations old it may surprise many that today's celebration, unlike St David's Day, is not an unbroken centuries-old nationwide celebration. It has more of the whiff of paint on road signs and hair-sprayed flicks than the smell of ancient boar sweat and wolf prints. Yes, the Dwynwen tradition tenuously outlived the zealots of the Reformation and Welsh Methodism, but how and when did it become a new tradition celebrated across Wales? Intrepid reporter that I am, I went in search of the anonymous tradition-inventor of St Dwynwen's Day.

All traditions were invented sometime. Some traditions were once foreign fashionable art forms which were left in cultural rock pools as the tide of fashion drifted away. This happened in Wales with the triple harp, for instance. And if a new tradition is invented then the anonymity of its inventor is seen as a mark of success, conferring on it a suggestion of mythic legitimacy and longevity. This was the trick Iolo Morganwg failed to pull off when he invented the Gorsedd of Bards. St Dwynwen Day's trick has been to resurrect an anonymous tradition, but the inventor too has remained anonymous and therefore the invention is all the more 'genuine'.

So, how was the modern St Dwynwen's Day invented?

If anyone can be credited with helping Dwynwen step out of obscurity and speak the modern Welsh of greeting cards, then it's the softly-spoken Anglesey writer, Jane Edwards.

Brought up in Niwbwrch (*Newborough*) on Anglesey, Jane was aware of the legend of Dwynwen from an early age. Local lovers would make romantic wishes with offerings of a cork spiked with a pin into Dwynwen's well at nearby Ynys Llanddwyn. Jane's cultured primary school teacher, W. H. Roberts, also taught his pupils the story of Dwynwen and the love poetry of Dafydd ap Gwilym in an age when that was not the norm.

'I forget the year', said Jane, 'but it was about 1965. I'd been asked by the producer, Ifor Rees, to appear on a St David's Day programme or something of that sort, with Gwyn Griffiths of the *Cymro* weekly paper, the Archdruid Cynan, and lecturer Nora Isaac, to talk about a place in Wales we like to visit. I spoke about Ynys Llanddwyn and the legend of Saint Dwynwen and it created quite an interest.'

From then on, Jane was asked to tell the story of Dwynwen on radio and in print.

'I became an unofficial spokesperson for Dwynwen in a way. But it wasn't a deliberate effort to create a "Welsh St Valentine's Day", as they say – although I'm very glad it's become that,' said Jane who has now returned to the mother island after living in Aberystwyth.

So unlike Iolo Morganwg's calculated effort to reinvent the Druids, Jane Edwards didn't start out with a deliberate blueprint to make St Dwynwen's Day a national holiday.

But Jane Edwards is being too modest. It's not a coincidence that it was she who was chosen to appear in Ifor Rees's programme nor, more importantly, that it was she who saw the beauty and the human need in Dwynwen's story. She was uniquely placed. I'd argue that if it wasn't for Jane Edwards then St Dwynwen's Day would not be celebrated today at all.

Jane Edwards strode into the Welsh literary scene of the early 1960s like a young woman wearing a miniskirt to a chapel. She rewrote the rules of sexuality and women in Welsh literature. Her early novels *Dechrau Gofidiau* (1962) and *Byd o Gysgodion* (1964) brought sex into Welsh literature in a way not seen since the hot love poetry of the great Dafydd ap Gwilym in the fourteenth century.

In her MPhil of 2008, Nia Angharad Watkins notes that Jane Edwards' novels portray the age of 'existential vacuum' as the focus of the woman moves from the hearth to her body. Her novels dealt with previously taboo subjects such as contraception and abortion. Professor Jane Aaron describes Jane Edwards as being the first *écriture feminine* in Welsh where the author must give honest expression to the urges, senses, emotions and experiences of the flesh which are unique to the female sex.

It was her fame and courage which made Ifor Rees's choose her to give some colour to his black and white programme. And it was her cultural upbringing in Niwbwrch, married with her ability and wish to express female needs, which led her to be so touched by Dwynwen's story and Ynys Llanddwyn as a location.

But why did Santes Dwynwen catch on? Why not Santes Melangell, the patron saint of animals? Or Sant Teilo, patron saint of apples, who could have lent himself to an Oktoberfest-type cider festival? And without a committee, well, how can you organise anything in Wales?

But maybe that's it. Maybe it's the fact that no one committee or government body or pressure group initially took it upon themselves to promote Dwynwen that gave it the anonymous legitimacy which allowed it to ferment in Welsh society. And Dwynwen's ageless appeal to lovers certainly helped propagate itself. The 1960s and 1970s were the summers of love after all – even in sliced-white-bread-munching Wales.

The media also played their part. With the launching of BBC Radio Cymru and Radio Wales in 1977 there was more need than ever for Welsh news items. Dwynwen's story fitted the bill perfectly.

If our universities were of true Welsh outlook they'd have degrees in 'Cultural Enterprise'. The degree would make use of the scribbled beer mats, badly-typed lobbying letters and the sheer determination, guile and experience of the generations of people who've diverted their energy to making Wales a country which is culturally richer ... though not made themselves materially better off. When such a course comes into existence (and why not? – it's surely more worthwhile than an economy built on the alchemy of the City of London), then the next stages of the invention of the Dwynwen tradition could be a module.

The Dwynwen story was too good to be left quietly fermenting in the cultural cellars of society. And *Cof y Genedl* (Nation's Memory), a Welsh history society, seem to have been the first to produce Dwynwen cards. The Society's founders were Edryd and Moelwen Gwyndaf, idealistic post-graduate students at Bangor. Newly-married with a baby daughter, Siwan, their flared trousers flapping in the winds of change, they produced Dwynwen merchandise for the 1977 St Dwynwen's Day.

Using the newly formed Gwasg Gwynedd printers (another enterprise started by young nationalists, the poet Gerallt Lloyd Owen and Alwyn Williams), Cof y Genedl printed 'Dwynwen scrolls'.

'Some 250 scrolls were published on a parchment-type material with love poetry written on them', remembers Edryd. 'There were four different poems, including I remember, "*Crys y Mab*". As Cof y Genedl, we believed it was a way of publicising what we thought was an important and exciting part of Welsh identity and history.'

So, at that moment two potent passions were fused: love for a person and love for a country. The protesters and activists with paint in their hands knew that if Welsh was to survive it had to be the language of romance as well as of road signs.

Dwynwen therefore became a fully-paid-up member of the Welsh Renaissance. This Welsh Spring in the 1960s and 70s saw a quite exceptional generation of young people change the face of Welsh culture, only to be stopped in their tracks by the failed referendum of 1979. This Renaissance could be compared to the Catalan *Renaixença*, but whereas any good guide book to Barcelona will discuss the Catalan Revival, the Welsh Renaissance is shamefully ignored.

The scrolls, and later other Dwynwen cards, were sold through the new informal network of independent Welsh-language book shops. One of the first of its kind, Siop y Pethe, was opened in Aberystwyth in 1967 by another idealistic young couple of the *Renaixença*, Megan and Gwilym Tudur.

Gwilym gives another insight into why he believes the Dwynwen tradition grew in popularity. 'Many people then and now feel their Welsh isn't good enough to write a love letter. The Dwynwen cards therefore give them the perfect opportunity to write some loving comments without showing their perceived linguistic failings.'

But despite making great gains in popularity since the early days, Dwynwen is still unknown to many, if not most, in Wales outside Welsh-speaking culture.

In many respects, the celebration of St Dwynwen as opposed to St Valentine marks the great split in Welsh society: not so much linguistic, but the split between the people of the village chapel and the people of the village carnival. The descendants of ministers and chapel-goers ('*Pobol Capel*' in Welsh) seem more likely to celebrate Dwynwen; the carnival people, St Valentine. It's the split between Welsh and mainstream Anglo-American culture. It's the difference between Sali Mali and Mickey Mouse; the Urdd and the Scouts; *Disc a Dawn* and *Top of the Pops*, even Plaid Cymru and Labour.

And while I understand that Dwynwen could never compete with the global capital and lure of Valentine, she doesn't seem to have won the hearts of those who are loud in their dislike of commercialism and globalisation either. After all, St Valentine's Day has as much to do with love and romance as the Xmas Sales has do with the birth of the Son of God. It's mostly tat for the tasteless. Why then aren't those with too much hair and a liking of purple clothes, or our worried warriors with the world on their shoulders, celebrating Dwynwen? For if ever there was a local, non-globalised celebration financed by what is, at best, a cottage industry, then Dwynwen is that. But, maybe Fairtrade is just for foreign goods? Maybe Dwynwen is just too difficult to get their tongues round? Dwynwen, it seems, may need to be more of a 'goodtime girl' and less of a good chapel girl if she wants to be better known.

As the poems of Dafydd ap Gwilym, a man who was a fan of Dwynwen, show, sonnets of smut, of mutton dressed as lamb, of romance and fancy words, are all part of the Welsh culture of courtship. Reviving Dwynwen from obscurity was a beautiful idea, for Welsh is a language of many things, but most of all a language for love.

Cambria, volume 11, number 4, December 2009

This article got me into hot water with Leighton Andrews AM. This was partly because the editor of Cambria had changed my more neutral title (below) to his more provocative, 'The Stalinisation of Welsh History'. If it taught me anything it was, don't ever use any article with the words Stalin or Hitler in it – you'll end up having a totally futile point-scoring argument which gets you nowhere.

The early years of the twenty-first century were quite a stressful and heated time. It was obvious to me that the Labour party had decided on a political strategy of making Welsh nationalists feel bad about themselves and undermining their intellectual confidence. It wasn't obvious to me, however, that Welsh nationalists knew how to deal with this.

Into this context came the competition to name the top 100 Welshmen and women. It soon became a proxy war for Welsh nationalism and British nationalism in Wales, which said much more about Wales in the first years of the Assembly than it did about the eventual winners and losers.

Two dead white men

An interesting question became the focus of intense debate on the web, newspapers, and television in 2004 – there was even a debate on the floor of the National Assembly in February. But perhaps the most interesting aspect of all is what that question revealed about Wales' contemporary political culture.

In 2003, culturenetcymru.com, which was set up to promote Welsh culture globally via the internet, decided to run a *100 Welsh Heroes* web-poll. It was well done – a smart website and effortlessly bilingual. The PR was effective, with items and updates on the voting on television and the newspapers. The site attracted nearly 85,000 votes from thirty-seven different countries and a staggering 3.5 million hits. For all the new technology, the idea was an old one, for in 1913, the *Western Mail* held a similar poll. The Edwardian Welsh voted for their Welsh heroes and Owain Glyndŵr was the winner. He and the other top heroes were celebrated with beautiful marble statues in the hall of heroes in the newly-opened Cardiff City Council chamber where, majestically, they still stand.

Things weren't quite so majestic this time round, however. In fact, the whole event became quite nasty towards the end. Despite the early lead by the crooner Tom Jones, it was a two-horse race between Owain Glyndŵr and Aneurin Bevan. The head-to-head between these two great Welshmen highlighted the big underlying, on-going *Kulturkampf* in Wales.

Bevan was declared winner on the 1st of March, beating Glyndŵr by 127 votes – it seems that Labour party members were in better order than Glyndŵr's modern emailers. But what struck me was the venom the anti-Glyndŵr camp displayed towards the historical figure.

What is going on? Maybe with the establishment of the Assembly in 1999 a new political and cultural space has been created. Welsh Labour, therefore, needed to find and promote a new Welsh icon to fill the vacuum which could be filled with a new Welsh sensibility. That is why Aneurin Bevan, more than ever before, has been promoted by the Labour establishment, in direct contradiction to the reality of an increasingly commercially-driven Labour party 'restructuring' his NHS.

But why such venom towards Owain Glyndŵr? Why does a fifteenth-century nobleman who led a national rising at a time when Welshmen were discriminated against in the church, and when Welsh people were not allowed within the walls of garrison borough towns like Caernarfon, Conwy or

Cardiff after sunset, create such hostility?

Aneurin Bevan was a charismatic, intelligent and clever man who was determined to alleviate the poverty and suffering he had witnessed as a child. For that, many of us are grateful. But the fight against poverty became mixed up with the fight against the Welsh language and Welsh identity, as if you couldn't have both. Aneurin Bevan was a good man and a gifted cabinet minister, but he was not unique. Had there been no Aneurin Bevan, there would still have been some kind of national health service. Even in post-war Germany, with the country on its knees, the conservative CDU governed for over fifteen years and built up a health service. The German system is different, of course, but when did you last see a sixty-year-old German showing traces of childhood rickets, and which country now has the better survival rate for heart disease or cancer?

In a speech in the Assembly chamber, Leighton Andrews, AM for the Rhondda, reminded the other members that Glyndŵr's parliament was 'not democratically elected, not gender-balanced' and that it was 'comprised largely of Welsh toffs'. The member from the Rhondda could also have added that Glyndŵr couldn't set the video either. I don't know whether Bevan was for gender equality (who does?), but I do know his Labour Party constituency was against a women-only list, in the true 'spirit of Nye Bevan'. More than being an adversary, Bevan, with his fine tastes, would, I am sure, have appreciated Glyndŵr's generosity at his home, Sycharth, famous for its fine hospitality and free-flowing wine – as Iolo Goch sang, '*na syched byth yn Sycharth*' ('and never thirst at Sycharth').

For a party whose slogan was 'education, education, education', Glyndŵr should be an obvious hero. In the famous letter to Pope Benedict XIII of Avignon written on 31 March 1406 from the church at Pennal near Machynlleth,

Glyndŵr outlines his vision of two universities for Wales, one in the north, the other in the south. Had Glyndŵr been successful, Wales would have had a university in the early fifteenth century that would have ranked among the first twenty-five universities in Europe. As it was, his rising was defeated and Wales, much to our detriment, had to wait some 470 years until the opening of the University of Wales college at Aberystwyth in 1874.

This aversion to Glyndŵr has diminished our understanding of the man and the national movement he inspired and led. There has been no revisionist, Marxist interpretation of Glyndŵr's war to compare with the assessments by other European historians of the great events from their pasts. The Welsh Labour movement hasn't embraced Glyndŵr in the same way as the Czech Left has chosen to interpret the battle of Bila Hora in 1620, where the Hussite Czech nobility was crushed by the forces of the Austrian Catholic Counter-reformation. And why on earth did Welsh serfs and Oxford students alike return from England to fight and die for Glyndŵr if he was just another 'toff'? There are very few really inspiring events in Welsh history, so why is the Welsh Labour movement so shy of studying and claiming one of the few interesting ones? Why does Welsh Labour find it necessary to be so *anti*-Glyndŵr? Jeanne d'Arc may not be a top icon for French left-wingers, but can they be said to be *anti*-Jeanne d'Arc? Are Czech left-wingers *anti*-Jan Hus because he didn't appear to stand for 'gender equality'?

Yes, both Bevan and Glyndŵr fought in different ways for their beliefs. Bevan, fought against the poverty of his family and community and overcame his stutter; Glyndŵr, the nobleman, gambled everything, and in addition to facing the constant threat of assassination, lost his family, his lands, his fortune, and his country.

On the day of the final result of the internet poll, Llew Smith, Member of Parliament for Bevan's old seat of Blaenau Gwent, said he'd be surprised if 'one in a thousand' people in Cardiff's Queen Street knew who Glyndŵr was. He implied that the outcome of Glyndŵr's struggle was irrelevant, while everybody had benefitted from Aneurin Bevan's career. Even in McDonald's-munching Queen Street, there is room to doubt Smith's 'one in a thousand' figure. It does help, of course, that there's a whopping great statue of Bevan at the end of the street. My only quibble about the statue is that it doesn't say enough about Bevan and his achievements. But if people are really so ignorant of Glyndŵr, doesn't that say far more about our education system than the man himself?

This 'who knows about?-ism' towards Welsh history, culture and literature is endemic in the rhetoric of a powerful grouping in Welsh political life. It celebrates philistinism, taking the lowest common denominator as a bench-mark. It closes down debate, castigates those with differing opinions as 'snobs' or 'middle-class'. But there's a deeper reason for the unease about Wales's history. Were people to engage meaningfully in cultural debate it would mean debating Welsh identity and language in an intelligent manner – a debate which would highlight the moral vacuum in the hearts of many of those most active in Welsh politics today. These are the people who constantly use the perceived threat of 'fascism' or 'racism' to deny the Welsh language political rights. The reasoning seems to run: 'because the Nazis killed six million Jews, Welsh kids can't have Welsh-medium education' or that Welsh can't be championed as a community language.

What of Bevan's legacy? Has it not spawned a political culture which offers traditional Labour voters a responsibility-free deal – you vote for us, and someone else, somewhere else, will pay more taxes so that you can have more for free? And why are so many of the 'Bevanites' so against Welsh self-government? Would Welsh self-government not have delivered Bevan's social agenda a generation before, rather than having to wait for the exceptional circumstances of 1945? This shows the tenacity of the Labour Party's British nationalism, in that many would prefer to live under a Margaret Thatcher or another English (British) Conservative than under a Welsh government of their own colour. There has, historically, been a minority view within Welsh Labour, such as the grouping around the unofficial *Llais Llafur* newsletter in Gwynedd in 1945, which advocated combining the social agenda with a positive one towards the Welsh language and Welsh constitutional aspirations. Aneurin Bevan, unfortunately, was never part of this group.

Because Glyndŵr's movement failed, Wales opened its new National Assembly almost 600 years too late. And, oh, how dismally it has failed to light the imagination! Has one celebratory poem, song or painting been created to mark the opening of the Assembly? The new institution has inspired no-one, or commissioned nobody, to produce works like the paintings of the opening of the first liberal pan-German parliament at Frankfurt's Paulskirche in the Springtime of Nations in 1848, or the iconographic images of the First Irish Dàil in 1919. There is no feel-good factor about the Assembly, and no amount of public awareness campaigning can change that situation if, at its heart, the governing party champions a man who was against the whole idea anyway.

This is a pervasive and long-standing colonial attitude. Imagine that Wales had suffered an edict prohibiting the naming of streets, squares or public buildings after Welsh national heroes. Would there have been any fewer streets or places named after our heroes than there are today? In the entire new Assembly complex in the Bay why isn't there even one location named after the one Welsh hero who actually died for a Welsh parliament?

In the nineteenth century we invested our energies building chapels instead of creating a civic Welsh identity. We wasted the twentieth believing that the choice was either to eradicate TB or to save the Welsh language. What is there to show for a century of proto-Bevanite agenda? Our language has been decimated. Economically Wales is, in relative terms, poorer now than in 1904; in the 1950s our GNP was twice that of the Irish Republic; in 2003 it was a staggering 30 per cent less. As the 'non-historic' nations of Eastern Europe joined the EU as proud, normal, sovereign states, Wales was rapidly being overtaken economically by countries like Slovenia, which only twenty or so years ago lay under the seemingly irremovable yoke of totalitarian misrule.

Perhaps, even more than it intended, the culturenetcymru.com poll created significant 'cultural debate'. By the use of modern technology the poll highlighted the cultural rift in our country between Bevan's people and Glyndŵr's people. With the Welsh public now advocating greater powers for the Assembly, is there a chance that this historic rift might not turn into an entente cordiale, promoting and preserving what is best of the aspirations of both Glyndŵr and Bevan?

In this 600th anniversary year of Owain Glyndŵr's parliament at Machynlleth, the internet threw some interesting light on a modern country with ancient voices.

Cambria, volume 6, number 3, May–June 2004

'The Things'

The BBC has in recent times done much for broadcasting in Wales and in Welsh – for some MPs, too much, even! However, it wasn't always so, and it is only because of the dedicated efforts of the far-sighted few on behalf of the many that Welsh-language broadcasting, and treating Wales as one unity, became the norm rather than the exception.

Like all institutions the BBC initially wheeled out the imagined 'boffin in a white coat' argument: that it was too technically difficult/advanced/expensive to broadcast in Welsh or directly to Wales. It's almost comical.

In the fast-changing world of information technology I believe we need some of the previous guile and determination to keep and increase Welsh and Wales's footprint in the media.

Battle of the Airwaves – early Welsh radio

It's the great historical misfortune of Wales that it is not an Eastern European country but rather a Western European one. Nowhere is this more clear than in the field of broadcasting, as the early years of radio and the struggle for Welsh broadcasting on the BBC confirm.

Truth be told, Lord Reith, the father of the BBC, was a grumpy soul. What's more, his 6' 4" frame not only towered over the development of radio in the UK but stood as a brooding scarecrow blocking the sunlight from the seeds of Welsh broadcasting.

Displaying the condescending arrogance which a certain type of Scotsman holds towards Wales, and the Welsh language in particular, he came out with some cracking snide remarks which today are amusing but which hardly show an appropriate level of gratitude to the Welsh people for their contribution through the licence fee to Reith's salary.

'Silly Welsh deputation' was his description of the

meeting held on 30 November 1928 organised by the registrar of the University of Wales to discuss the possibility of providing Wales with its own station. He hadn't changed his mind two years later when the same deputation met to discuss the same issues. 'I had three hours with some perfervid Welsh at the University,' he wrote in his diary. 'Their criticisms were extraordinarily ignorant,' he added with the usual put-down the British establishment historically uses to cover up their colonial attitude.

Yes, the story of Welsh broadcasting is of the guerrilla warfare of letter-writing, soggy petitions and lightning attacks in public meetings and boring committees. For, although the UK as a state was one of the world-leaders in radio broadcasting, Wales as a nation was not. This is the story of the at-times-bitter campaign to give Wales its moral right in the revolutionary new medium: a campaign that created the modern Wales, as Dr John Davies says in his excellent and very readable history of the BBC, *Broadcasting and the BBC in Wales* (to which I'm greatly indebted).

The concern about the lack of programmes in Welsh had grown throughout the mid 1920s. By 1927 the Departmental Committee of the Board of Education noted that 'the present policy of the BBC is one of the most serious menaces to the life of the Welsh language'. It was with this background that the first regular Welsh broadcasts were made, not from Wales, nor even England, but rather Ireland.

The first of the Dublin programmes was transmitted in April 1927 and they continued regularly until March 1928. As none of the Welsh offerings of British stations had been broadcast at fixed times, those from the Irish capital were the first regular programmes of Welsh interest. There was nothing clever about the programmes – they consisted mostly of songs sung by the Welsh residents of Dublin and by the crews of the Holyhead ferry boats. The programmes were arranged by W. S. Gwynn Williams, who founded the International Eisteddfod at Llangollen after the Second World War. Their amateurism if anything underlined the fact that broadcasting wasn't some hidden science, as Reith and his colonialists seemed to imply, but was really quite a straightforward affair. The Irish Free State, which even in the height of the Depression had a GDP of less than half that of Wales, had only four years earlier come out of a economically disastrous War of Independence and Civil War. Yet the Irish Free State could set up its own radio service on 1 January 1926. This only highlighted the ridiculous cap-in-hand situation which Wales found itself in. That their service also included broadcasts in English and Irish wasn't lost on campaigners for a Welsh radio station.

The broadcasts in Welsh from Ireland were referred to in the report *Welsh in Education and Life* which was published in August 1927 and which I mention above. As the report tartly notes, 'it is a rather pathetic comment on the position of Welsh in its own country that the only regular Welsh programme is that given once a week from the Dublin station of the Irish Government.'

The Report and the Irish broadcast thrust the issue of broadcasting in Wales onto the political agenda, where it has been virtually continuously since then, and where the excuses and tactics used in the 1920s and 30s reappear time and time again as if the issue of broadcasting were some political *Groundhog Day* re-run.

The response of the BBC to the Report inflamed people. The director of the Cardiff station, Appleton, rejected the call for news and science programmes in Welsh. 'The BBC has taken as its official motto "Nation Shall Speak Unto Nation" and this would be merely empty bombast and oratory did the nation not seek to use a common language for this interchange,' he reasoned. That the Welsh nation may wish to speak unto itself in its own language was evidently a notion which hadn't entered Appleton's head. Moreover, he went on from being myopic to being patronising with the words, 'Let us reserve for Welsh broadcast nights gems of poetry and immortal songs: let us have – as we have had – her preacher poets on Sundays and let us have her music.'

Such nonsense was not acceptable to nationalists whose aim was not to reserve Welsh for any one sphere of activity, but to make it the natural medium of daily life in Wales.

With pressure mounting, in early 1928 Appleton invited respectable Welsh societies to nominate representatives to a committee which he formed to offer guidance on Welsh programming. The 26-member Welsh Advisory Committee persuaded Appleton to relax his ban on spoken (as opposed to sung) Welsh, and on 21 March 1928 the first *Welsh Interlude* was broadcast, a fifteen-minute talk given by Ernest Hughes – one year after the Irish programme!

The next six or seven years saw the heat of political battle turned up, especially so since the newly-formed Plaid Genedlaethol Cymru (later known as Plaid Cymru), under the leadership of Saunders Lewis, recognised the importance of the new medium and made it a campaign issue. Saunders Lewis himself in 1929 threatened that 'thousands of Welshmen' would be prosecuted for refusing to pay their licence fees if the situation didn't improve. Foreshadowing the tactics used by Cymdeithas yr Iaith Gymraeg forty years later in their campaign for S4C, some younger members of the party advocated blocking transmissions and receiving court prison sentences.

As well as threats of action, the wide campaign by the nationalists for a Welsh service, and a Welsh national service in both languages, aimed to undermine the quack-science arguments by Reith and his cronies. In 1930, E. G. Bowen, a physics student at the University in Swansea, tried to undermine the BBC's technical excuses. He set out to show how Wales could be better served by two transmitters within Wales (rather than the BBC's proposed two in the English West Country) which he believed would enable 97 per cent of the population of Wales to receive programmes specifically designed for them. In 1932 Bowen also suggested setting up what would today be called a 'pirate radio station' on board ship outside the three-mile limit. In fact, Bowen became such a nuisance to the BBC that he was even given his own secret service-type 'Bowen file' and was regarded by Reith as a 'bumptious young man' – which was rich coming from Reith.

The geography of Wales was regularly used as an excuse against providing a Welsh service, but it became an excuse too far. When a new transmitter for Scotland was opened in 1932 in Falkirk the BBC made their excused that the mountainous nature of Wales made it impossible for a comparable arrangement to be made in Wales. 'Everybody knows,' J. E. Jones of Plaid Genedlaethol Cymru commented sarcastically, 'that Scotland is flat'.

Apart from the Welsh language, the big ideological fight with the BBC in those early years, and which was woven into the argument about the location of transmitters and identity, was the BBC's insistence on creating a broadcasting service for what it romantically called 'King Arthur's Land' (the West of England and southern Wales) against a national service for Wales as a country.

The radio campaign in Wales was therefore two-pronged. On the one hand was the 'cultural nationalist' agenda which was purely to increase the hours broadcast in Welsh; on the other was the 'political nationalist' agenda to create a fully Welsh (Cymreig) service: that is, a national service in Welsh and English – a Wales Broadcasting Corporation if you like.

The latter campaign had at its vanguard Saunders Lewis, a person some propagandists have mistakenly painted as being against any manifestation of English-speaking Welsh identity. In 1933 the man who had re-learnt Welsh as an adult wrote: 'What we mean by a Welsh national programme is an all-Welsh programme every day for every part of Wales, as well as an English programme based on Welsh national consciousness, in exactly the same way as the present programmes are based on English national consciousness.'

And in 1935 he said: 'We do not propose that the people who cannot speak Welsh should be either ostracised or ignored. On the contrary, I say very emphatically that their interests . . . as English-speaking Welsh people [must] be adequately served'.

The various campaigns by groups, petitions (one which began in the mining towns of Gwent), Plaid Genedlaethol Cymru, dignitaries, the University Advisory Committee and Saunders Lewis in particular, proved partly effective, and in the spring of 1935 the BBC created a Welsh Regional service – and with that, closed the first battle in an ongoing campaign for Welsh identity on radio and what could be a nice ending to this article. But it's not, because the perspective is very different when Wales is seen in an Eastern European context.

Were Wales located to the east of Germany she would as a country today be ratifying a treaty of entry into the European Union as a proud and normal sovereign nation state, and not play-acting being a nation with its Ruritarian Assembly. There is a special patronising attitude by Western countries specially reserved for East Europeans based on bar-room humour towards diacritic-written languages and funny countries ending in '–ia'. And, of course, there's the 'ethnic wars'. The West Europeans have ethnic wars as well, but at least they have the good manners to have their ethnic wars far away in America, Africa and Asia, or have two really big ones and call them grandly 'World Wars'. And unlike Western Europe, today not one East European nation suffers the indignity of her native language hovering above extinction, as is the case in Wales or Brittany, where you can't buy a loaf of bread in your own language in your own country.

We're always told how well Wales, and Welsh, is treated. But that's only because we compare our status with that of other Western European languages, like Breton, which is unlucky enough to be in the French Republic. Many, if not most, of the states which denied or obstructed broadcasting in indigenous languages in the 1920s and 30s were located in Western Europe: Britain, France, Italy, Spain – not the East. Even in the 1930s Stalinist USSR there were more programmes broadcast and more status given to indigenous languages than there are in France today.

The facts are revealing. Estonia began its regular broadcasts in its own language on 18 December 1926, and in 1927 it was broadcasting more programmes in Esperanto than the BBC broadcast in Welsh. Latvia, a country with a similar number of native speakers as Wales, set up its own Radio Central in 1924 and began broadcasting on the 1 November 1925. When the Welsh were still poncing around and haggling to broadcast news in their own language, the Croatians (who a dozen years earlier were up against a nasty policy of Magyarization) were producing their own 15-minute news bulletins from May 1926. Across the Black Sea, even Georgia, where the Caucasus Mountains would no doubt have caused a *petit mal* for BBC engineers, were broadcasting in 1927 not only in Georgian but also Russian, Armenia and Azeri – a full year before the BBC relaxed their ban on spoken Welsh.

What is more incredible is that not only were all these

states poorer in terms of GDP than Wales, but they had all suffered damaging and bloody wars – the Great War, revolution, wars of Independence and even civil wars – on their own land (as had the Irish Free State), which crippled infrastructure and the exchequer. And yet, they were still broadcasting proudly whilst the Welsh, in their British ignorance, had the nerve to look down on these faraway countries of which they were so proud to know so little.

Maybe the comments by the superintendent engineer at BBC Broadcasting House, Cardiff, in 1928 weren't so off-the-mark after all. In that year, the Welshman J. P. K. Williams was denied promotion because, as the superintendent engineer explained, he 'Did not consider that the Welsh temperament [was] as suited to supervisory duties as the English temperament'.

In the light of our lack of determination to take control over our own wavelengths compared with our Irish and East European friends, maybe he was right.

Cambria, volume 5, number 6, Autumn 2003

Another little-known history, but a wonderful story and one I read as a passing comment in a book by, I believe, my former lecturer at Aberystwyth, Dr John Davies,

I have so much respect for old warriors like Glyn and Hawys James. It wasn't easy at all being a Welsh nationalist after the war, when people and politicians would casually make the link between the campaign for Welsh-medium education or Welsh-language broadcasting, and the Nazi gas chambers. What I also particularly like about the activists of the 1950s is that, unbeknown to them, a great dawn of Welsh identity and confidence was just around the corner. We can see that now, but it was in no way obvious to them – and still they fought on. It says a lot about the morality of these people that they decided to believe in a minority political and cultural view when they so easily could have gone with the grain on mainstream British culture.

I also like the fact that the radicals of the 1950s were always so tidily dressed. When did people begin to believe that to be radical you had to dress shabbily?

Radio Ceiliog!

Come closer, I'll tell you a story of a radical, illegal voice, a wireless 'samizdat', the voice of a radio-free Wales at the height of the Cold War. I'll tell you the story of some unsung heroes of Welsh broadcasting, people now in their seventies or eighties, who should be awarded BAFTAs. Have a good look at this man, Glyn James, and his wife, Hawys, of Ferndale in the Rhondda. Don't let their age deceive you – they're more radical than many an armchair *New Statesman* rebel or wannabe Valleys Boy Hero refighting the Ebro front on the banks of the lazy Taff.

This is the story of Wales's first political pirate radio

station which spluttered onto the airwaves over forty years ago.

The prosperity of the 1950s saw a growth in radio and television ownership, with half the households in Wales paying for a TV licence by 1959, but there wasn't a corresponding growth in broadcasting *from* Wales, either in Welsh or English. There was even suspicion towards developing a Welsh broadcasting service in the 1950s, with some Labour MPs such as George Thomas complaining that the BBC in Wales was 'corrupting the minds of the Welsh people' with what he saw as a Welsh nationalist bias – a rather incredible assertion, unless *any* broadcasting through the medium of Welsh or nod to Welsh nationality was assumed to be nationalist propaganda.

Against this background Plaid Cymru was being denied its party political broadcast because of a classic Catch-22 directive which allowed Party Political Broadcasts to parties with fifty Westminster candidates or more. Wales had only thirty-six *constituencies*! This created a rather difficult situation for Plaid Cymru, a party that would, quite obviously, put up candidates only in Wales. One can, perhaps, imagine a young, enthusiastic, irredentist member suggesting that they stand and reclaim the historic and formerly Welsh-speaking lands of northern England, *Yr Hen Ogledd*, and fight Catterick South (indeed, one can't imagine that the Plaid vote there could have been much worse than in most parts of Wales at the time). With a background of frustration at the stop-go attitude to Welsh broadcasting with the state forcing a political blackout, Plaid members took the law into their own hands. And this is where the old warriors Glyn and Hawys James come in.

'We'd heard that the SNP were broadcasting from a pirate radio station, and so I drove to Kirkintilloch near Glasgow to learn more,' remembered a young-sounding 81-

year-old Glyn James. The plan was simple, to cut across the transmissions from different masts in Wales and broadcast the illegal Radio Cymru/Radio Wales. The first transmission took place in the winter of 1958 from the garage of Gruffydd John Williams in Gwaelod y Garth, a hill-top village near Cardiff.

In those days, the BBC television service shut down at 11.00 pm. Just before close-down the pirates would break into the transmission and tell viewers not to switch off. The radio programme would then commence at 11.00 on the same frequency, transmitting over a distance of some seven miles and for about ten or fifteen minutes. The transmissions were in Welsh or English or both, depending on the area. The programmes were a home-grown mixture of political news, propaganda and song – Glyn remembers that *Ar Lan y Môr* and *Men of Harlech* were particularly popular. The songs were sung live on air by pirates, at which point Glyn called on Hawys, hovering in the background, to sing the station's jingle. Now, once again, Hawys bursts into song, singing jingles which haven't been heard for forty years, simple little ditties to the tune of 'Hey ho, hey ho, it's off to work we go':

> Stay tuned! Stay tuned!
> Don't switch off your TV,
> This is your choice to hear Wales' voice
> From Plaid Cymru, Plaid Cymru!

Or:

> Stay tuned! Stay tuned
> To Plaid Cymru
> You'll hear good news and different views
> From Plaid Cymru, Plaid Cymru!

And then in Welsh:

Gwrandewch! Gwrandewch
ar Radio Cymru!
Yn seinio'n gref drwy wlad a thref
Yw'n neges ni!

The first broadcast was a success and was followed by cups of tea and Welsh cakes prepared by Gruffydd John Williams's wife, and it was 1.30 a.m. by the time the outlaws decided to pack into the Singer car and return to the Rhondda. Despite the good humour and camaraderie of the first broadcast, this was no joking matter. To be caught breaking into a transmission could lead to a £200 fine and two years in jail.

Driving home after that first broadcast, with the transmission kit in a box on the back seat, the car was ordered to stop by a policeman in Nantgarw. After winding down the window they heard with great relief and astonishment that the policeman was simply asking for a lift to Pont-y-pridd. Glyn obliged, and with Hawys and Anita Williams giggling in the front, he suggested the policeman made himself comfortable on the 'parcel' on the back seat and to ignore the 'slightly tipsy ladies' in the front seat.

From that time, there might be two or three broadcasts a week from different venues across Wales and outside. Safe houses were used. Returning from broadcasting in the West, Glyn would drop off the kit at the coal shed of the Reverend Dr Gwilym ap Robert of Addol-dŷ in Glynneath before making for the Rhondda, where he feared he was under suspicion and faced being caught. From the start the radio pirates were also suspicious that their phones might be bugged, so, the transmission kit was duly code-named 'y ceiliog' (the cockerel) to avert suspicion, and Radio Ceiliog came to be the nod-and-wink name for the clandestine 'station'.

Dr Gareth Evans, a mathematician at Swansea university college, made two or three 'ceiliog bach' for distribution, and as Radio Ceiliog spread its wings, the press, and the authorities, were keen to find out more. During the Caernarfon National Eisteddfod of 1959, a local Fire Brigade officer, Jim Parry, was in charge of the ceiliog, and made sure the surveillance vans from Manchester sent to catch and prosecute the offenders were miles away in Llanberis Pass when the transmission took place from Twtil in Caernarfon.

Plaid members in London were also keen to get in on the act and to take the message to the heart of the British establishment. Working closely with some of the big names of the time who were Plaid supporters and members – Meredith Edwards, Rhydwen Williams, Ray Smith, Hugh Griffith – Radio Ceiliog succeeded in breaking across a Party Political Broadcast by the Conservative Party, making the point loud and clear. Features followed in the *Manchester Guardian, Daily Express* and *Time & Tide* magazine.

Closer to home broadcasts were made from the farm of Morgan 'Mwcyn' Williams on the top of Penrhys in the Rhondda (before the modern housing estate was built). 'Mwcyn was an old farmer who enjoyed a few pints of cider at the Duke of York in Tylerstown,' recalls Glyn. 'he would ride down on his horse, and the horse would carry him back up! One bitterly cold evening with ice on the ground, I noticed I was being followed by two suspicious Labour Party aldermen. They left their car at the end of the drive and walked the few hundred yards to the farmyard, at which point I switched on my headlights full-beam and Mwcyn let his dogs lose. The aldermen fled and slipped on the ice – they didn't bother us again!' giggles a gleeful Glyn James, recalling these 'Keystone Cops' antics.

Nobody was ever prosecuted for broadcasting Radio Ceiliog. That may well be down to good fortune and a touch of good sense by the authorities. 'Maybe they thought we'd get too much publicity if we were caught and jailed,' Glyn suggests. The broadcasts finished in 1962, by which time Plaid had won the battle for representation on air and Wales was winning representation as a televisual nation, borne out by the opening in 1967 of the confident BBC headquarters in Llandaf. In no small part these successes were down to now largely-forgotten pioneers like Glyn and Hawys, the poet Harri Webb and the educationalist Dafydd Orwig, as well as Gwynfor Evans, who always understood the importance of the media. At the other end of the scale stood members of the Broadcasting Council for Wales, and a man with the Darth Vader-like title of 'Controller Wales', the six-feet-five Alun Oldfield-Davies, whose patience and determination towers over the history of broadcasting in Wales.

Compared with the useless young generation of the early twenty-first century, with its sneering irony, its self-obsession and self-indulgence, it is heart-warming to listen to people like Glyn and Hawys speak with such commitment and passion and yes, *hwyl*, about politics. They weren't obvious candidates (who is?) for breaking the law. Glyn was the fourth of eight children of a poor family in Llangrannog, Ceredigion. He had little education before moving to the Rhondda to work with the Coal Board. Hawys was born and bred in Ferndale, and despite her name, she didn't speak Welsh until she learnt it as a student in Barry Teaching College.

In the currently prevailing – and dominant – Welsh political historiography, the 1950s is a time both of Cold War and cosy conservatism, before the flowering of revolution, idealism and hope in the 1960s. But the Wales of that time saw a powerful subterranean stream of radical ideas and deeds which flowed beneath the parched land of officialdom and of the Establishment above it. From the tentative emergence of the '56 Group' of artists to the first voices of the self-conscious political Anglo-Welsh poets, the foundations of the Welsh Revival of the 1960s were being laid by brave pioneers who risked imprisonment and ridicule to make the voice of Wales heard above the dismal droning of Jacobin 'One Nation' conservatives. Nowhere was this truer than in the field of broadcasting and in the spirit of people such as Glyn and Hawys James and Radio Ceiliog. These were people who almost willed the Welsh nation into existence. For the rebels of Radio Ceiliog, politics was as radical as it was invigorating. Their actions also raised the fundamental question underlying the whole project: 'Why should Welsh people have to campaign for Welsh broadcasting in the first place?'

Cambria, volume 5, number 5, Summer 2003

This was another passing comment which lit my interest. I remember hearing an interview with Meredydd Evans on John Hardy's Saturday morning programme on Radio Cymru, 'Cofio' (remembering). I was driving down the Prom in Aberystwyth on a beautiful Saturday morning and thinking, 'wow – that's it. That's a cultural eureka moment. The whole 'Song for Wales' event encapsulated the excitement of the 1960s in Wales, a 'can do' generation'.

It was also an excellent excuse for me to write an article about Meredydd Evans – a man who has contributed so much to contemporary Welsh culture, and to our understanding of traditional Welsh culture too.

A Song for Wales

'Thank the Lord, we are a musical nation', for quite unintentionally the crowning of Prince Charles as the Prince for Wales in 1969 set up a new Welsh musical institution. You've all heard of the Eurovision Song Contest: well, the Investiture played a small part in setting up *Cân i Gymru* (the 'Song for Wales' contest) and Wales' participation in a musical Celtic Unilateral Declaration of Independence.

The Student Prince's pageant of peasants and protests took Wales the closest it's been in centuries to civil war. But the peacock empire's spectacle gave voice and focus to a Singing Revolution, where the language of the chapel became the voice of change.

At its centre, conspicuous but not centre-stage, was Meredydd Evans, father of *Cân i Gymru*. Now ninety years old but with the strong noble look of Caractacus about him, his life and career encompass a breadth of experience which I doubt any Welsh generation will be able to match for decades to come. Raised in the slate-quarrying village of

Tan-y-grisiau to the sound of his mother's folk songs, he was, like many prominent Welshmen, a Conscientous Objector during the war. Ubiquitous in the 1940s, he sang with the much-loved post-war Triawd y Coleg, appearing in the popular series of Welsh *Schlagermusik, Noson Lawen*. His love of song and erudition led him to meet and marry an eminent American opera singer and musicologist, Phyllis Kinney, and by the 1960s he was Head of Light Entertainment at BBC Wales. Although no long-haired teenager, he was a man with a burning ambition to place Welsh-language pop music in the mainstream of Welsh life.

As Commissioning Editor, Meredydd Evans (or Merêd as he's known to all) had overseen the broadcast of *Disg a Dawn*, based weakly on the BBC's popular music show, *Top of the Pops*. But his ambitions for Wales were greater. He wanted Wales to sing her song in sequins and mini-skirts in the increasingly popular Eurovision Song Contest – the annual televisual event which brought an exotic glamour to the uncentrally-heated homes of 1960s Wales, with songs of denied lands and lands which now no longer exist.

He made enquiries in 1965 and 1966 as to whether Wales could be represented and compete as a nation at the Eurovision, citing our own unique language and musical tradition. However, he was told that the BBC, as the only recognised state broadcaster, was responsible for the one entry from the UK. But, that wasn't the end of the song.

In 1968 *Disg a Dawn* launched an annual song competition, and in 1969 along came the Investiture – the red rag to the Red Dragon. Men were marching, bombs were being planted, families were being split. It gave Merêd an idea.

'There was plenty of money available to celebrate the Investiture,' he remembers from his home in Cwmystwyth. 'So, we took advantage of this and set up *Cân i Gymru* – a

'Song for Wales' competition. There were six programmes and we received some 700 songs for the competition! A hell of a lot of them were about Charlie and I made sure not one of them got through! Not that they were any good in any case – they were stomach-churningly sycophantic, *chwydlyd*.'

Eventually, the 700 were weeded down to thirty, and the historic winning song for the first *Cân i Gymru* was 'Y Cwilt Cymreig' – a historic song, though not the best Welsh song ever. It was sung by young Margaret Williams of Anglesey – who is now, in best Eurovision Song Contest tradition, something of a gay icon.

The first ever Song for Wales competition, having been motivated by the Investiture, came into contact with an unlikely request from Republican Ireland in 1970. An Irishman, Con O'Connell, was keen to set up an Interceltic Music Festival at Killarney in County Kerry. Con got in touch with Merêd and Phyllis.

'We decided to combine *Disg a Dawn* and *Cân i Gymru* into one competition. The first winner of the newly amalgamated competition in 1970 was Eleri Llwyd (who is now the wife of Elfyn Llwyd MP) with 'Nwy yn y Nen'. It was, and still is, a great song, but it unfortunately came second to a Scottish group in Killarney.'

Merêd's 'baby' has become a regular feature in Welsh music and is broadcast every St David's Day with all the fun and Byzantine politics of the European voter phone-in. Like all phone-ins, there's predictability about it. In the Eurovision, Greece always gives 'douze points' to Cyprus; in *Cân i Gymru* familiar composers get votes of mutual back-slapping size from the audience. Piano-playing school teachers from the Welsh-speaking areas can likewise rely on Hellenic-style *Enosis* support from friends and family, whilst the unknown from the un-mental-mapped south-east are as likely to win as Armenia is of voting for Turkey; they smile excitedly to the camera, innocent that they are dead men walking.

But for all the failings of *Cân i Gymru* and the Interceltic Festival it still beats the Eurovision Song Contest, which has descended humiliatingly to having to 'ironicise' itself to be accepted. It's like a fat woman deliberately dancing the belly dance to get noticed . . . in an 'ironic' way of course. It's unedifying. It's humiliating to European culture and once proud nations, the culture of the Nations of Springtime now in the autumn of their lives. Like mutton dressed as lamb or people speaking posh when they answer the phone, it's just embarrassing.

In the Newspeak of mass-culture, which it helped foster and which has now devoured it, 'international' means *sans* national. 'Multinational' means to sing in one language, not many. It's not even amusing any more. Once a schoolchild's yearbook of 'foreign people and places', it's all become an out-of-town retail park of music. Not even the guilty pleasure of cultural prejudice, once suppressed like farts, has evaporated as most singers sing in English.

If the BBC were serious about winning the Eurovision they could opt for the Stalin UN-style option. You'll remember that Stalin, having killed maybe 10 million Ukrainians in the *Holodomor*, felt a pang of Ukrainian patriotism during the formation of the United Nations and insisted Ukraine and Belarus be given seats (and unswerving pro-Soviet votes) on the new body. Why not make Merêd's dream come true and give Wales and Scotland Eurovision independence, then? Owing to the English Diaspora in Wales and possible reciprocal votes, it would give an almost certain 'douze points' every time for one of the Britannic nations!

Maybe I am too cynical (ok, I am), but would we *want* to compete at the Eurovision? The other option is for Wales to take more seriously events such as the Interceltic festival in Killarney. They may not be as glamorous nor widely known, but similar festival such as *Liet* in Friesland and *Blas* in Inverness do have integrity . . . and are more interesting. But then, integrity isn't glamorous.

The Welsh genius is to adapt, translate, and colonise musical forms from the Italian triple harp of the seventeenth century, which we made our own, to sea-shanties, hymns, Handel's *Messiah* to rap and pop. And maybe, in a world of global culture, of which we're an integral part, that's all we can aspire to now. But I feel something is being lost in the Welsh singing world today.

Despite today's bravado, Welsh singing is suffering from a lack of self-confidence. The new wave of sweet-smelling young mixed-sex choirs give the impression of a healthy tradition, but how many of them are now part of that tradition and could sing a 'traditional' Welsh tune? When the last of our sweaty, blazer-wearing Male Voice Choirs fade away in twenty years' time, who will sing our hymns and *Lieder*? What will have replaced them? Songs from the musicals (the Babycham of music) for telly votes; American gospel (but never the true soulful music of Russian orthodox church or Russian folk music) for 'passion' and modern compositions, as unlistenable and unloved as they are ubiquitous, for the judges? Like Robert ap Huw transcribing the last golden droplets of harp music from the courts of our princes, should we not now save the best of Welsh choral music before it is lost in the Eurovision of choral music?

Our Assembly seems too shy or too downright embarrassed to promote or finance Welsh music or arts. The Irish Republic's Arts Council in 2005/06 spent £10.72 per head of population on the arts. Wales spent £8.80. Where money has been spent, priorities have been skewed: Adam Price MP felt the full-force of the fat lady sit on him when in

July 2009 he questioned the cultural priorities and strategy of the Welsh National Opera. Price noted that our national opera company has never appointed a Welsh Musical Director or staged a Welsh opera. Adam's argument wasn't against the WNO staging foreign operas. He wasn't advocating, as some implied (often with snide remarks about Welsh culture which betrayed their scarcely disguised colonial view of Wales) *Hywel and Blodwen* on loop. His argument is simple: where's the national platform and support for a Welsh Dvořák or Sibelius?

The National Opera's budget is £6.3 million of the Welsh Arts Council's money. But the budget for the 'traditional' Welsh music foundation, Trac, is £274,000. I'm certainly not arguing for cutting the Opera Company's budget, but rather increasing the money given to forms of music which are played only in Wales.

With the current recession and the talk of slashing budgets, some politicians predictably want to ring-fence the budgets of health and education. But we're a People, not pupils or patients. If any budget should be ring-fenced then it surely must be Heritage. At the moment the budget for 'Heritage, Sport and the Welsh Language' is a mere £160m – less than 1.5 per cent of the Assembly's budget. When I read that hospitals like Addenbrooke's in Cambridge spent £190,452 on food which was wasted in one year, I can't believe that Welsh hospitals aren't also as wasteful. Moreover, any saving in Heritage is neither here nor there in the Assembly's £16bn budget.

Forty years after the first *Cân i Gymru* arrived we've taken two steps forward but one step back. In being rejected from one institution, Eurovision, Meredydd Evans, with others, created an alternative one, so maybe being accepted by the mainstream isn't always the best option nor outcome for a culture or an artist. Mêred's *Grundgesetz*, basic law, like thousands of others is, 'popeth yn Gymraeg' – everything in Welsh. Through the National Eisteddfod's 'Welsh only' rule and the elasticity of the Welsh language, we've converted all musical forms into Welsh. But are we in danger of being a culture of translation? Is it that deep down we really are just too embarrassed to sing as Welsh people?

It makes you almost wish the House of Windsor and a subaltern mother-loving MP had another Investiture to get the juices flowing again!

Cambria, volume 11, number 3, September–October 2009

It's all in context of course, but in comparison with the general public I'm a rabid Germanophile. I'm always thrilled to see the daily newspapers from across the German-speaking lands laid out before me in a German train station or kiosk. While I was in Siop y Pethe in Aberystwyth that I realised that, in our own way, we had the same experience in Wales with the phenomenon of the papur bro *– and here, once again, the name of Meredydd Evans, a great Welsh cultural entrepreneur, turns up as the instigator.*

The papurau bro *tick enough government-approved targets to make a bureaucrat weep with joy. However, like all good ideas, they began with a dream, and if you will a dream it will happen.*

They're certainly something to be proud of. But I'd also like to suggest that some forty years after their foundation our papurau bro *may need to move up a gear to face the changes in Welsh society and reading habits.*

It's not heavy... it's my bro

I suppose it depends how you buy your copy of *Cambria*. If you are one of those people who picks it up at what is called a 'Welsh-language bookshop', then you'd probably have seen them. You may possibly have seen them peeking shyly from behind more glossy publications in garages and newsagents in the more Welsh-speaking parts of Wales. They're the *papurau bro*, a term which is rather thinly and insufficiently translated as 'monthly community papers'. In fact, they're a cultural phenomenon.

A visit to Siop y Pethe or the Inc bookshop in Aberystwyth reminds me of those train stations in German cities, where the daily regional papers of the far corners of the country are laid-out with justifiable pride. In Siop y Pethe, rather than the *Süddeutsche Zeitung*, the *Berliner Morgenpost*, the *Frankfurter Neue Presse*, you'll see *Yr Angor*, *Y Tincer*, *Papur Pawb* and *Y Ddolen*. These are the *papurau bro* which serve just the old cantref of Penweddig (that is north Ceredigion, around Aberystwyth). Other towns will display the local *papurau bro* for their region, and the stronger Welsh is locally, the greater the number of publications.

The *papurau bro* have played a pivotal rôle in the renewed confidence in the Welsh language by giving people a reason to read Welsh. At a time when established Welsh publications like the weekly *Golwg* and *Y Cymro* sell around 5,000 copies, the total sale of all of Wales's fifty-two *papurau bro* totals around 70,000. That's one in six of all Welsh-speakers. But despite the high sales figures not one person is employed by a *papur bro*. The strength, and weakness, of the *papurau bro* is that they're all published by a dedicated network of some 2,000 amateurs.

To understand the phenomenon of these papers it's important to get to grips with the concept of the Welsh '*bro*'. In Breton the same word means 'country' or 'land', but in Welsh it's more nebulous – part geographic, part historical, part cultural and part emotional. Sometimes it may even represent a cluster of villages or an area which shares the same accent. Many of the papers cover geographical areas united in the popular imagination for centuries: for example, *Y Ffynnon* is aimed at a readership in an area some 15 miles in length, from the river Glaslyn, east of Porthmadog, to Dwyfor, east of Pwllheli, corresponding with the local medieval *cwmwd* of Eifionydd. Now you won't find Eifionydd on any map, and the *cwmwd* (commote) as a unit of local government hasn't been a recognised political entity since Owain Glyndŵr called his parliament at Machynlleth in 1404, when he summoned two delegates from each of the dozens of *cymydau* (commotes) of Wales.

The cymydau *and* cantrefi *of Wales*
Published by permission of Prifysgol Cymru/University of Wales

Somehow, the concept of the *cwmwd*, even if people don't recognise the word, has lived on as a sign of a tenacious popular folk memory. It has survived the failure of Glyndŵr's intifada, the imposition of counties through the Acts of Incorporation of 1536 and 1542, through the Land Reform Acts of the nineteenth century, and the local government reorganisations of 1974 and 1996. For the next local government reorganisation, at least in rural areas, the *cwmwd* would provide an excellent ready-made entity. *Cymydau* invariably correlate to the same drive-to-work circumference so central to modern-day town and country planning. The *cwmwd* is an entity smaller and closer than the county and far more useful and meaningful than the pretty pointless units designated under 'Community Councils'.

But back to the *papurau bro*. Interestingly, the first *papur bro* wasn't founded in Gwynedd or Ceredigion, but in Cardiff. The founder was the great Welsh nationalist and internationalist, Meredydd Evans. In May 1972 he sensed the need for a medium to bring together the growing Welsh-speaking population of Cardiff. By 1973 he and a dedicated band set up *Y Dinesydd* (The Citizen). *Y Dinesydd* was distributed around the new Welsh-medium schools, the chapels and other locations where Welsh-speakers congregated like exiles, but in their own capital! Uniquely, it was distributed free of charge.

Within a year four other *papurau bro* had been launched: *Papur Pawb* (Everyone's Paper) for the Tal-y-bont area north of Aberystwyth; *Llais Ogwan* (Ogwen [valley]'s Voice – spelt with the local pronounciation of Ogwen) for the Bethesda area in Gwynedd; *Clebran* (Chatter) for bro Y Frenni in north Pembrokeshire; and *Pethe Penllyn* (Penllyn Culture: literally '*y pethe*' ('the things') refers to Welsh-language culture) for Penllyn (yes, another *cantref*) in the Llanuchwllyn area near Bala. In a wave of can-do excitement, twelve further *papurau bro* were launched in 1975–76 and fourteen more in 1977–78, all from money raised locally, all maintained by committed individuals, all inspired by the vision of seeing Welsh-speakers reading Welsh and by the desire to reinforce the particular Welshness of the '*bro*'. Many of the initial helpers were newly-graduated students from Aberystwyth and Bangor, many straight from the sit-ins and law-breaking of the Welsh road signs campaign, or inspired by the passion behind the radical Welsh-language group Adfer, with its Russian back-to-the-land populist-inspired ideas. The *papurau bro* were a tangible sign that Welsh was losing the shackles of being the language of only the chapel and the kitchen.

Considering the political background of many of the people associated with the movement, it was ironic that within a few years, the *papurau bro* were being attacked for being too conservative and safe. In an article in the weekly national magazine *Y Faner* in 1983, Plaid Cymru MP and now Presiding Officer of the Assembly, Dafydd Elis Thomas, castigated the *papurau bro* for not reflecting any 'sign of modernism in Welsh culture or the new political consciousness needed to sustain it'. This was not quite true: *Papur Pawb* campaigned in 1990 against the 'Education First' movement which sought to dilute the Welsh-medium provision of junior school education in Dyfed, and *Llais Ogwan* gave the front page of its first edition to explain the new Common Land Registration Act. Dafydd El's attack fell on mostly deaf ears. For, despite the odd campaign, the papurau knew their audience and their rôle. *Papurau bro* weren't meant to be radical agitprop mouthpieces. The true radicalism of their continuing success was the *normality* of their content: deaths, marriages, new-borns, a photo of the winning local darts team, maybe an article by someone who's been abroad, or congratulations to someone passing the piano Grade One examination. Yes, this was information deemed too trivial at times even for local newspapers – the radicalism, simply, is that it's all in Welsh.

By 1990 the growth of the *papurau bro* reached a plateau, and questions were asked about the future direction of the movement from a commercial as much as from a political perspective. In a report commissioned by the Welsh

Cooperative Movement in that year, Dr Emyr W. Williams raised the feasibility of shifting the movement up a gear and establishing weekly *papurau bro* which would employ people. Once again, the movement's innate conservatism and localism, militated against this. By the 1990s the *papurau bro's* inability to grow and strengthen their economic base led many to do what would once have been unthinkable – to go to the state for financial support. Since then, most *papurau bro*, if not all, have received some state sponsorship through the Welsh Language Board. In one respect, it's good to see the state supporting such important cultural expressions, because one copy of *Y Gambo* will say more about Wales than the entire repertoire of the Welsh National Opera has ever done. But, at a time when publishing has never been easier or cheaper and when there is more disposable income than ever, dependence on state hand-outs is a sign of weakness. A Welsh language culture hooked on state support will end up moribund, like some Finno-Ugric people have within the Russian Federation.

Today, there are fifty-two *papurau bro*. The design of some can still look as rough as those early copies literally cut and pasted together by committee over a kitchen table, with cups of tea and bara brith to keep the troops going. Some are still folded together in a '*noson plygu*' (an evening of folding the printed pages together into completed copies) – a gathering which reminds one of the tweed-making sessions of female crofters in 1930s Harris. Too many papers still contain too much information from a dwindling segment of Welsh life: for instance, the 'news from the chapels', which does little more than repeat verbatim the contents of chapels' own internal newsletters. This is a dubious and unreliable barometer of Welsh language strength and activity (especially in the south-east) which is often given a disproportionate degree of space – and is invariably the sign of a weak culture.

The best *papurau bro* are those who cram in local news combined with interesting articles about local history or engaging characters. Less successful are the ones which try to be high-brow, with articles apparently composed by retired school mistresses. The most notable and positive development of late is that the BBC's daily Welsh language web service, *Cymru'r Byd*, now publishes a selection of articles extracted from *papurau bro*. But the movement has failed to develop on its initial success and go on to creating glossy colour publications, as the Basques have managed with their own versions of the *papur bro*.

Supporters of the *papurau bro* can be rightfully proud of their movement, but too many are in danger of slipping into complacency. The *papurau bro* face a challenge. In many instances, the papers are still put together by the very same people who launched them thirty years ago. The baton has not been passed on – either because the 'pioneers' won't make way, or because younger people are unwilling to rise to the challenge. In many areas *papurau bro* are too closely associated with the older generation. Whole pages given over to obituaries are a touching elevation of the ordinary and local, but also represent a somewhat depressing mirror-image of a vanishing core of older readers.

There are also questions about the very concept of the *papur bro*. In an increasingly mobile world, is the concept of a homogeneous cultural *bro* as valid as it once was? Is it not perhaps too local, if not too ethnic, even for a Welsh-speaker who has newly moved into the area?

These questions are nowhere more acute that with the *papurau bro* of Glamorgan, and in particular with the first one, *Y Dinesydd*. Does the inability of a Welsh-language publication to sustain itself in the most affluent and now most numerous Welsh-language community indicate the structural weakness of language in that community? Or, is it a symptom of the very concept of the *papur bro* being incompatible with an urbanised, city community? Or perhaps the paper is not local enough? Rather than there being a *papur bro* for the whole of Cardiff, should there not be one for Canton or Whitchurch and other suburbs? Moreover, should there not be a monthly, if not weekly, Welsh-language newspaper for Cardiff? Oh, for the passion, commitment and can-do attitude of those pioneers of the 1970s!

With so many *papurau bro* now over forty years old there are good reasons to celebrate – but no reasons to be complacent.

Cambria, volume 7, number 4, July-August 2005

Good songs touch us personally; great songs move nations. 'Yma o Hyd', written in 1983 by Dafydd Iwan, then an iconic singer, more recently President of Plaid Cymru, was the right song at the right time. Maybe surprisingly, it's probably more popular now than it was almost thirty years ago. It goes to show how a once minority view of Welsh history and society has become mainstream … it's also a great song to sing!

Wales' Singing Revolution

'Do you remember Macsen? Nobody knows of him, one thousand six hundred years is too long a time for the memory . . .'

Yes, well, that's my loose translation of the opening verse of a Welsh song you'll hear at the Llanelli Scarlets rugby games, Welsh home football and rugby internationals and a few late-night drinking sessions. The song is Dafydd Iwan's famous and rousing, *'Yma o Hyd'* (Still Here!).

It doesn't quite sound right in English; translation can be a little like sex with the condom on. 'Still here' suggests you're still waiting for the number 25 bus into town on a wet Tuesday evening; *'Yma o Hyd'* has more of the 'I will survive' grit in it.

The song is but one of many in a long line of rousing, patriotic songs which is the musical backdrop to what could be called Wales's Singing Revolution. But *'Yma o Hyd'* is also different. More than any other song it signifies a public decision taken by a section of the Welsh nation on which course to take at a pivotal fork in its history. It was the song which, in fact, changed Welsh history.

Until the Welsh Language Act of 1967, Welsh had no official status in her own country. Some concessions had been won, but the Welsh language still lived under the shadow of the 1536 and 42 Laws in Wales Act (or Acts of Union). The Laws stated: 'The [Welsh] people of the same dominion [England] have and do daily use a speche nothing like ne consonant to the naturall mother tonge used within this Realme' and then declares the intention 'utterly to extirpe alle and singular sinister usages and customs' belonging to Wales. In other words, positive discrimination, big-time, in favour of the English language.

Dafydd Iwan was a leading light of Cymdeithas yr Iaith Gymraeg (the Welsh Language Society) formed by the baby-boom hope-smiths in 1962 in reaction to Saunders Lewis's rousing 'Fate of the Language' radio lecture. Cymdeithas yr Iaith was there to reverse the pernicious effects of the Acts of Union and reverse the downward slide of the Welsh language.

Dafydd was also one of the first young people to self-consciously sing modern songs in Welsh. After all, why should Welsh people sing other people's songs in other people's language? His acoustic guitar style of singing became the jukebox to the Welsh revival, spawning other similar individuals and groups. He was Bob Dylan without the pseuds or Victor Jara without the guns.

But much of this national awakening, the 'long 1960s', if you like, came to a stop in 1979 when Wales voted overwhelmingly against a national assembly. And that's where Dafydd Iwan's 'Yma o Hyd', composed in 1983, comes in.

In so many ways, Wales was a different country thirty years ago. A time when a cup of coffee meant something instant and nasty and definitely not cappuccino; where dual carriageways were littered with people with their heads under bonnets fixing bust gaskets or other faulty engines, where men still smelled of body odour and thought it 'poofy' to use aftershave (hell, where men still *used* words like 'poofy'). There were still some 20,000 coalmines in Wales and thousands of steelworks and the Soviet Union seemed destined to rule for a thousand years.

But 1979 came like a meteorite thumping into Welsh soil. The newly-elected government of Margaret Thatcher, coupled with the economic shock of the world oil crisis, led to thousands being made redundant. And the whopping 'No' vote in the Referendum for a Welsh Assembly in 1979 was a kick in the stomach for the national movement – a deep feeling of betrayal. Wales, it seemed, had voted itself out of history: a rare case of a nation conducting national euthanasia.

The reaction was of depression and anger among Welsh nationalists. It led some people to look to more radical ways of defending Wales. The Arson Campaign – Meibion Glyndŵr's burning of English-owned second homes – which began on 12 December 1979 was one. Some on the radical fringe of Welsh nationalism aimed to combine the cultural with the industrial struggle. It saw the establishment of groups like WAWR (Workers' Army of the Welsh Republic, also serendipitously soft-mutated Welsh for 'dawn') and the Welsh Socialist Republican Party.

Other Welsh radicals like those of Cofiwn, the National Commemoration Association, took a slightly different view. Their interpretation of the failure of 1979 was that the Welsh people were ignorant of their glorious past when Wales was a land of Princes, not just proletariats. Cofiwn became more active producing pamphlets, posters and processions – and also drew the attention of the Special Branch.

In March 1980, sixty people across Wales were arrested as part of 'Operation Tân' in a bid to find the Meibion Glyndŵr arsonists. All were released, but the ugly event is commemorated in Dafydd Iwan's 'Sul y Blodau' song.

Another Dafydd Iwan song, 'Ciosg Tal-y-sarn', is a satire

on the police's bugging of a public telephone in the village during the same turbulent time.

The Welsh Language Society's present general secretary, Dafydd Morgan Lewis, was a student at Aberystwyth then, and remembers trying desperately to grab 'any blade of grass of hope'.

Some campaigners, like Edryd Gwyndaf, remember trying to put on a brave face. 'You'd try and rationalise things: maybe Saunders Lewis was right, that to have independence or a parliament before the language was revived (like in Ireland) could be detrimental to the language; maybe 1979 was too early and we weren't ready as a nation; maybe the historic mission now was to win status and strengthen the language, before constitutional change. You felt that Wales was dying so every Welsh rugby win was important and every new Welsh-medium school a little victory.'

In this tense atmosphere, in 1982 the 700th anniversary of the killing of Llywelyn ap Gruffudd, the last native Prince of Wales saw over 1,000 people gather at the commemoration stone in Cilmeri near Builth Wells. Was Wales becoming like Northern Ireland?

In 1980, the year before the famous Irish H-block Hunger Strikes, Gwynfor Evans, Plaid Cymru's first MP, had made a stand. He threatened to go on hunger strike if the Conservative Government didn't hold true to their election manifesto promise to deliver a Welsh-medium television channel. Had the Conservative's Iron Lady not made a famous u-turn on the issue, then it's not difficult to imagine that Wales would have become a very nasty place indeed. In fact the first S4C broadcast on 11 November 1982, ironically (or was it?) exactly a month before Llywelyn's 700th anniversary and that Cilmeri rally, offered a rare glimpse of hope in a pretty depressing period.

'It wasn't a good time for Welsh nationalism', recalled Dafydd Iwan. 'It was depressing and things didn't look as if they'd get any better. But I remember Dafydd ap Tomos, who ran a chip shop in Pen-y-groes near Caernarfon (and who now runs Oriel Plas Glyn-y-weddw on the Llŷn peninsula) telling me he liked my songs but they were too melancholic, too much looking back, and that I should compose something which celebrated that we were still here as a nation.

'I remember composing '*Yma o Hyd*' in the attic at my house in Waunfawr near Caernarfon, and I remember having the idea; it was so simple, and yet, hell, it struck a chord,' he recalls from his Recordiau Sain office near Caernarfon – the record company he co-founded in 1969.

In 1982 Dafydd Iwan had been on a morale-boosting tour with the professional Welsh folk group, Ar Log. The tour marked the 700th anniversary of Llywelyn's death at Cilmeri, and the theme tune of the tour had been the yomping '*Cerddwn Ymlaen*' ('We will walk on'). Dafydd Iwan's brain began ticking.

He told me, 'I remember someone once asked Gwynfor Evans, "If you were to put a date on it, when would you say the Welsh nation was born?" Gwynfor answered "383 AD". That was the year Macsen Wledig (Magnus Maximus) the Roman general in charge of Britain left 'Wales' and returned to Rome, essentially leaving us to fend for ourselves. As 1982 had been the 700th anniversary of Llywelyn's death, then 1983 could be the 1,600 anniversary of the founding of the Welsh nation. It was a simple message that despite everything we were still here as a nation a thousand and a half years later.'

And that's where I think Dafydd Iwan's song changed Welsh history. OK, not by itself, but it was the wake-up call. To continue the Roman theme, like brave king Caradog

(Caractacus) it told people to march through Rome and ignore the torments of opponents and sneers of the crowd. As Barack ap Obama said in his inauguration speech in 2009, 'Starting today, we must pick ourselves up, dust ourselves off, and begin again the work of remaking Wales.' After all, we're in the shadow of the most powerful language the world has ever known: it is amazing that there's anyone still speaking Welsh!

Dafydd Iwan's decision to use anniversaries is a popular strategy in all political campaigns, but it takes a special ability to recognise when to make those anniversaries count. Hardly anybody in Wales in 1982 had heard of Macsen Wledig. This was no Llywelyn or Glyndŵr. It would take the understanding of Gwynfor Evans to produce a pamphlet, once again like a little Dunkirk ship to save the troops, this time on Macsen Wledig, to raise some public awareness of the man. It took another genius to understand that 1983 was the year that Wales needed to look for the positive and aim for the possible and have some self-confidence back.

In this respect Dafydd Iwan followed in the tradition of Saunders Lewis and his decision to set on fire the training camp and aerodrome for the RAF at Penyberth in Llŷn in 1936. The decision by himself, Lewis Valentine and D. J. Williams to set Penyberth on fire was in many ways arbitrary. Saunders Lewis decided that the 400th anniversary of the insult of the 1536 Act of Union had to be remembered in some way to raise morale and make a point. He was determined to prove that not all people in Wales were compliant subjects of the 'realm of England'. Penyberth offered that anniversary.

Dafydd Iwan didn't strike a match: he struck a chord, which sang through Wales.

In 1983 the Welsh Language Society began their campaign for a second Welsh Language Act. The cross-party

Campaign for a Welsh Assembly (later Parliament) began in 1987. Coincidentally, both the Act and the Assembly were achieved exactly a decade from the beginning of their campaigns. Bit by bit, things were slowly changing.

The Miners' Strike of 1984 also brought many people together, creating cross-party and non-party networks which would become valuable in the successful 1997 devolution referendum. Eighteen years of Conservative rule, when Wales hadn't voted Tory, also did much to win people over the cause of an Assembly for Wales. But Wales had changed more fundamentally than that. After all, the north-east of England hadn't voted Tory either, but voted resoundingly against having their own assembly in 2004. The difference was the 'national' in the National Assembly. '*Yma o Hyd*' was the cultural ballast to the ballot box vote.

At an important junction in our history '*Yma o Hyd*' made a decision and thousands of people sang that decision into life. It was a decision that we would will ourselves into being as a nation and that nation would have a Welsh-speaking heart.

It's almost obvious now, but it could have gone the other way. After all, Ireland's Great Emancipator, Daniel O'Connell, although himself a native Irish-speaker, thought the language was a burden or encumbrance and advised people to change to English. Wales may have been reborn in some way in the 1980s, but not necessarily with the Welsh language at its heart. After all, there was a strong argument that the 'fear' of the language played a big part in the success of the No vote. One could easily imagine a scenario where a nascent 'progressive' Welsh nationalist movement could have decided to degrade the Welsh language in the name of 'national unity'. '*Yma o Hyd*' made sure that there would be no Welsh nation without the Welsh language, and it helped keep intact the unity of the Cymry Cymraeg (Welsh-speaking Welsh people) as a political as well as cultural concept. '*Yma o Hyd*' became a second anthem and has even been adopted by many small local football and rugby teams.

But '*Yma o Hyd*' is similar to the national anthem in another way too. For me, like our anthem, it's almost too defensive. The anthem's final line is '*O bydded i'r heniaith barhau*' (oh, long may the old language continue). Does '*Yma o Hyd*' also suggest that just 'continuing' is good enough? Is that as good as it gets? 'Surviving'? 'Continuing'? 'Still here'?! Not 'flourishing' or 'expanding' or 'growing'? But like '*Yma o Hyd*', the anthem was written following a body-blow to the language – the publication of the 'Blue Books' in 1847. It wasn't until 1852 that the contents were translated into Welsh and so became public knowledge. Is it more than a coincidence that it was in 1856 that the anthem, with its slightly defensive last line, was composed; and likewise '*Yma o Hyd*' after the 'No' vote?

In 2036 Dafydd Iwan, if he's *yma o hyd*, will be ninety-two years old. If he's still writing, and like Saunders, looking for an anniversary, may I suggest he, we, write another song?

May I suggest that on the 500th anniversary of the Acts of Union we set ourselves a target to totally erase from our forehead the dent caused by 500 years of the pointed finger which says 'Taffy, know your place'?

May I suggest that we make Wales a proper nation and a nation where a majority of people can once again speak Welsh?

Then we won't just be '*Yma o Hyd*', but singing a new song.

Cambria, volume 11, number 6, June-July 2010

A patch of land

I say I'm from Cardiff (Caerdydd), but I have by now lived more years of my life in Aberystwyth. Still, the lure of the city is strong and it's of great regret to me that I don't have a Cardiff accent.

Growing up a Welsh-speaker in the city in the 1970s and 80s was to feel very much the internal exile. I remember my friend, Rhisiart, gazing towards the mute estates of Pentrebane and shouting 'Wake up!', though it was fifteen years before Catatonia sang 'Every day when I wake up, I thank the Lord I'm Welsh'. However, whilst it's possible for language enthusiasts to over-egg the strength of Welsh in the city, it certainly is a different place compared to when I grew up there. The increasing 'Welshness' of Cardiff – both linguistically and culturally – is one of the most hopeful and exciting developments in Wales in centuries.

It's exciting to be able to play a part in a massive historical project, to make the city the first truly Welsh capital. Every time I return to Cardiff I'm amazed with another 'that wouldn't have happened when I was young' jaw-dropping type comment as I see Cardiff grow into the capital of a new state and become a warmer house for the Welsh language.

The Capital

Maybe, against the odds, Cardiff was always destined to be a capital. Just like the capital cities of the other Three Countries, it is located in the south east. Moreover, doesn't its primary river, Taf, share the same etymology as the Thames (*Tafwys*) both originating in a pre-Anglo-Saxon and pre-Roman *Prydain* when the whole of Englandandwales spoke ancient Welsh?

Cardiff is certainly the lucky city of Wales. It voted against the Assembly in 1997 but still got the Assembly building. It was one of the most anglicised parts of Wales but still became the centre of both Welsh-language and English-language broadcasting, despite the fact that a large proportion of its population don't even tune into the Wenvoe mast located on the city boundary.

But as the historian John Davies notes, it was the growth of Cardiff and the ambition of its city elders which led the city to define a concept of a civic Wales even if only to further their own civic egos – better to be the premier Welsh town than just another middling English one.

In that very tradition, Cardiff is now the capital of 'corporate Wales': the Wales which has grown with the Assembly, the bland Wales of 'Communities' with a capital C and 'development officers' working for bodies with coincidentally bilingual acronyms, where Wales is the new geographical expression, a brand, a Wales where Caernarfon is £61.90-@-34-pence-per-mile-from-Cardiff-ville – not the port of *Fflat Huw Puw* or *Cofis*; a Wales where 'minority aware' civil servants are hostile to the Welsh language in the name of 'equality'. But then, as every Gramsci-quoting Marxist-cum-capitalist will tell you, as he merrily quaffs like one of Gerard ter Borch's *Cavaliers*, this is the inevitable and necessary 'march through the institutions'. And so it is.

But, with the exception of the international rugby and, lately, football match days, nothing has done more to foster Cardiff's position as capital of Wales than the media. Certainly in little more than a generation Cardiff has mutated from being the capital of south Wales to the capital of Wales – a cultural and political shift that has been to the benefit of the city, and of Wales. It has become the undisputed capital for the Welsh-speaking community (that 'audible minority', as the poet Grahame Davies calls them). Caerdydd is now their El Dorado. For many a young person from Môn or Ceredigion, Cardiff is everything – where famous people have affairs and where every weekend is an international weekend. The place where, ever increasingly, they can speak their language just as much as they did back home, in regions which have become more English as Cardiff has become more Welsh.

Locating the media in Cardiff has led to the city dominating the visual landscape of Wales and perhaps obviously because of S4C, especially the Welsh-speaking community. In a quiet moment over a *cappuccino* one can muse on how different our visual landscape would have been had Swansea been the chosen capital. Although it may be somewhat ridiculous within a UK context, Cardiff is for the Welsh-speaker *'y ddinas fawr ddrwg'* ('the big bad city') – which rather contradicts its own promotion of itself as a small, accessible city. But for a linguistic community which is still largely rural, Cardiff is certainly the big smoke compared to Llangefni or Tregaron.

Thus it was that Cardiff became the New Yorkesque setting of *Bowen a'i Bartner,* the S4C 1980s detective series where the orange buses of Cardiff Corporation took on the same iconography as the yellow taxis of the Bronx. In *Dinas* the 1980s big-shouldered, smouldering soap of greed and sex of the Thatcherite years, Cardiff, is the Dallas of Wales. *Y Bae,* a series about the political and sexual goings on at the soon-to-be Assembly was a crisp moment in time. It captured the post-1997 euphoria of a nation reborn and captured an optimistic 'Thank the Lord I'm Welsh' Cardiff.

Not to live in Cardiff during the final three years of the twentieth century was to stand outside in the drizzle looking in at a Viennese State Ball, nose stubbed against the condescending condensation of the window looking at the beautiful people waltzing. How things have changed!

Caerdydd looms large in Welsh-language pop, and *'Cyfryngis'* (Welsh for media-types, from *'cyfryngau'* – 'media') are regularly lampooned in Welsh songs. Welsh-speakers from Cardiff are still treated with suspicion by many fellow-*siaradwyr*. Cardiff Welsh-speakers are different from other Welsh-speakers; they don't have the smell of rotting-flesh and a dying culture about them. They seem too happy and content – still a suspicious habit for a language unsure of its future in a culture nursing a Methodist hangover. The community is caricatured for its perceived lack of commitment to the 'cause' and for making good money on the back of Wales. To go to Cardiff, our capital city, is to 'sell-out', a funny state of affairs, and possibly unique. This perception is not helped by the unwillingness of so many of Cardiff's Welsh-speakers themselves to take sides or create a culture independent of their wages. Cardiff Welsh-language culture is at its most exciting and challenging in the hands of people who've learnt the language in adult life – and without them Welsh in the capital would wither on the vine.

The Cardiff accent in Welsh, if not much loved, is increasingly the accent of the young and urbane on S4C. On the English-language media, the Cardiff accent in English is either treated as a quaint novelty or as suggesting a hard, streetwise but good-at-heart-character – a Welsh version of the Cockney. It's an accent of those still not deemed acceptable enough to read the news, even the sports news. Even more ridiculous, the English accent of the capital is still not considered 'Welsh' enough by its own speakers, though to outsiders it seems very Welsh. And when 'the Valleys' are portrayed on the media, such is the pull of the capital that it's those Valleys that geographically feed into Cardiff that are portrayed – the Rhondda or Taf, very rarely the Ebbw or Llynfi.

Viewed through the prism of 'UK-ness', Cardiff is a nice but nothing-special city which, with the exception of international rugby matches, has less on-screen presence than provincial English cities.

For all the talk of the Cardiff of the *crachach* and middle-class, its own aesthetic is lower-middle-class, with aspirations so low they barely show above the pavement, a capital where the opening of the twelfth Ikea department story in the UK was celebrated as a badge of statehood, a capital whose population actually believes that the pokey, Lego-like Mermaid Quay is the height of continental sophistication. Oh for a gigantic crane, ball, and chain to flatten it and start afresh! Even as the seat of government in a devolved Wales, it is a capital with little political edge. Despite its awesome Millennium Centre and flourishing arts scene, Cardiff's political edge still hasn't managed to set the cultural agenda in either Welsh or English. However, Cardiff does lead in life-style, and maybe for the generation of the mid noughties and for the self-righteous non-voters that's more important. Cardiff offers life-style in a Welsh context. Cardiff is our decadent Tel Aviv to the Jerusalem of the Welsh tradition of language and class struggle.

But, whatever its faults, the historical process which is playing out in Cardiff today on the streets and screens is an echo of a process which took place among the Slavic and Baltic nations of Eastern Europe a century ago. Wales is an Eastern, not Western, European nation. Wales is Estonia, Cardiff is Ljubljana, the Taf is the Vistula. It's not 2005, it's still 1905.

Cardiff is the battle-ground of two historiographies. One is the reality of modern Wales forged as a white Victorian colonial culture, part of the great pan-English-speaking white colonial world – a New Zealand, Australia or Canada in the rain, the sluggish culture which has made us the most irrelevant and ignored part of Britain. Against that historiography is the truth of Wales as a small non-historic colonised European nation – to employ Engels' definition. A nation which failed, or was forbidden, to take the right turning at key stages in its history – Cilmeri, Glyndŵr, the Treachery of the Blue Books, 1979. It is the latter historiography and culture which offers Cardiff a future as a true European capital.

This is the battle fought literally street by street over the very names of those streets. Crudely, it is a battle between a Six-Generation history whose Welsh historiography goes only as far back as the period of the signing of the Treaty of Waikaito in 1863, and where anything earlier is the history of turnip-munching peasants and tribal warfare. Against it is a historiography of two millennia where Ifor Bach's kidnapping of Earl FitzRobert in 1158 is but yesterday, and *tribannau* were sung on Llandaf bridge.

But in its failures and frustration, Cardiff is our future. In an age where the rural community is transient whilst the urban is sustainable, maybe cities are where the future lies for the Welsh language and Welshness. Although not the ideal for the Welsh speaker, it's certainly better to be part of 10 per cent of the population of a large city like Cardiff, than 40 per cent of a small village. For the under-represented, non-Welsh speaking Cardiffian, it is the exciting comfortable city-state whose prestige straightens their backs.

For the ethnic minorities, Cardiff offers a challenge of confronting two identities, Welsh and British, to add to their first, whether it be Somali, Pakistani or Irish. A challenge which offers the alternative of not just continuing as yet another 'ethnic minority' of a small British city, but to form the vanguard of a shift of historical proportions – to become the first ethnic minority cultures to side with the minority language and culture indigenous to their host country, Wales: to create a culture embracing two colonised communities, one which would be as dazzling in its audacity and majesty as in its morality. For there can be no future for Welsh as a 'white only' language any more than there is a future for it as a part of 'Englandandwales'.

Cardiff has always been on the cultural cusp in Wales, a Roman, later Norman, then English garrison town built to quell and rule the native Welsh and literally keep them outside the town walls, a town Iolo Morganwg accused of being an 'alien community which aped English manners'. But then as the proud Cardiffian and Assembly Member, Owen John Thomas, revealed in his MA thesis on the subject, Cardiff was, until the 1830s, bordering on being a majority Welsh-speaking town, with four of its seven Nonconformist chapels holding their services in Welsh. As late as 1891, 67 per cent of the population of Llysfaen (the ugly-sounding 'Lisvane' in English) spoke Welsh. Welsh is the only language which has been spoken continuously in Cardiff since before the Roman stones of Cardiff castle were laid.

Cardiff is both a strength and a threat to the Welsh language – a creator of an urban Welsh language culture and a sapper of young people from the west. Its Welsh is also not the authentic Welsh of Rhydaman, Aberteifi or Gaerwen – a fact which Cardiff-based bodies like the Welsh Language Board and the Assembly shouldn't forget.

Despite the dangers, the animosity, the love-hate relationship, for me at least there is something mythical about the very word '*dinas*' (city) which Cardiff, Caerdydd, captures. With its roots in the word for 'hill fort' it binds us to our Celtic cousins in the 'duns' of Dundee, Dundalk and Dinard. It is a word of hope and beauty, and in Cardiff we have the excitement of building, daily, a young capital and creating our own Welsh civic aesthetic on screen and in sound, in bricks and books.

Caerdydd is the future – if only it knew its past.

Cambria, volume 7, number 2, March–April 2005

Although I speak no Breton I feel more affinity with, and understanding of, the Bretons than the Irish or Scots.

I really do feel that the disgraceful treatment of the Breton language by the French state and her supporters is a slight against my own family. The history of Brittany during the Second World War is one which is still used by the French as a stick to beat the Bretons with, even now when they have only the most minimal of rights.

In the same way, it was used by some against recognising the right of the Baltic states to independence from the USSR in the late 1980s . . . overlooking, of course, the greater evil perpetuated by nation states like Germany and Russia, which they had no problem in recognising.

I'll just offer the conclusion that some people don't like small nations and small languages. It's an affliction which affects those who wish to associate themselves with glory and grandeur ... a Napoleon national complex, if you like.

In any case, I'm proud of the contribution many Welsh people have made in fighting in support of the Bretons. I knew Delwyn Phillips, another old warrior, whose company I enjoyed a lot. He cycled from Pontypridd to Llandudno to find work during the Depression and used to take a daily swim in the sea off Aberystwyth late into his old age. His story was one I had to tell.

I'm even more impressed with the Bretons who've stood up to the French state.

The Battle for Brittany

2009 saw the seventieth anniversary of the beginning of the Second World War. In the national narrative of the British state it was the Great Patriotic War. For most in Wales it was a 'just war'. However, it is a much more awkward event for many other small nations.

These are the nations of Eastern Europe, caught between Hitler and Stalin as they chanced their dice fighting with one side or the other, desperate to retain some semblance of independence from the claws of the two genocidal dictators. But how many of us know of the fate of Wales's cousin, Llydaw – Brittany? And, maybe more pertinently, as we debate and deliberate the War – how would we as Welsh people have acted were we in their predicament? For the history of the Nazi occupation of Brittany from 1940–44 is a tragedy in more ways than one.

Gwenno Piette was born and raised in Aberystwyth and is the author of the University of Wales Press's *Histories of Europe: Brittany – A Concise History*. Her family's story throws an interesting light on this largely forgotten story . . . a story which still divides Breton society.

Gwenno's father was Arvel Piette, a Breton patriot who settled in Aberystwyth after the war. He was loosely associated with a handful of Breton nationalists and patriots who fled, sometimes for their lives, to Wales or Ireland following the 'Liberation'.

Arvel was born Jean Piette in 1920 in Lille in north-eastern France, the son of a non-Breton-speaking Breton mother and a French father. In his late teens Jean learnt Breton, adopted a Breton name, Arvel Even, and became involved in what the Bretons call the Emsav ('renovation'), the national movement for Breton rights. At the outbreak of the war he found himself studying botany at the University of Rennes, the capital of Brittany.

The situation of Breton was dire. Lessons in Breton were prohibited in schools: in fact, the French Education Minister, M de Monzie, succinctly announced in 1926 that 'for the linguistic unity of France, Breton shall be exterminated'. Breton was prohibited on Radio-Rennes. There was no status for Breton in civic life at all. And it wasn't as if there had been no call for such recognition for the language – a language spoken by an estimated 1 million people, many of whom were monoglot Breton-speakers.

Many Bretons had not forgotten the betrayal of the ideals of men such as the poet Yann-Ber Kalloc'h (the c'h in Breton is pronounced as the Welsh 'ch'). Like our Hedd Wyn, Yann-Ber was killed in battle in 1917. An estimated one million Bretons were drafted to fight for France (out of a total population of some 3 million). Tens of thousands of them spoke no French; a quarter of them never returned – the highest ratio of any 'region' of France. Like the Ulster Unionists, Yann-Ber thought that at the end of the war the French would recognise the sacrifice and faithfulness of the Bretons and reward them. He drew a petition intended to be sent to the Paris government asking for Breton and Breton history to be taught at school. Yann-Ber didn't live long enough to be disappointed. Many, however, like the Marquis de L'Estourbeillon, did. The Marquis even made requests to the Peace Conferences of 1919 and to President Wilson himself for status for the language, only to find his pleas fall on deaf ears. For, it seems, unlike the Ulster Unionists, being faithful servants of the state didn't bring the Bretons any rights. It is no surprise, then, that a section of Breton society believed in 1940 that the Germans couldn't be any worse for Breton culture and language than the French. It was a belief which was to cost them dear.

In many respects the 'tactical mistake' of a section of Breton nationalists was the same mistake as that of the French army – they both fought the last war. Where the French invested their hope in the Maginot Line, some Bretons invested theirs in the old adage used by the Irish, 'My enemy's enemy is my friend'. Some Breton nationalists (some eighty individuals, according to one estimate) actively collaborated with the Germans to try and promote independence for Brittany within a larger German Reich. Thousands more kept their heads down, but grabbed the relative linguistic freedom of Nazi occupation to promote Breton language and culture.

Although never a prominent player, Arvel knew many of the leading names of the period and played his part in promoting the language he had come to love. Writing under various noms de plume he contributed articles to Breton magazines and even assisted with the historic Breton language broadcasts on Radio Rennes-Bretagne. Amazingly, Breton had never been broadcast on French radio – it was the Nazi occupation that made it possible. Radio Rennes-Bretagne/Roazon-Breiz broadcast programmes in French and in Breton, and under the leadership of Roparz Hemon by June 1943 there were broadcasting daily for an hour or so.

Arvel's use of noms de plume and his relative low prominence meant he escaped the post-war 'justice' meted out to many similar Bretons. At an annual Breton language summer school shortly after the war, Arvel met Mair Phillips, Gwenno's mother. Mair was originally from Pontypridd but had moved to Birmingham to work at her brother Delwyn's drapery. Delwyn's home became something of a safe house for Bretons following the war. Delwyn helped Yann Fouéré and Gildas Haffrennou (Gildas was the son of Taldir, a well-known Breton nationalist who was in gaol) to escape from Brittany by offering work as a tailor to 'Claude Gwinamann' – Gildas's assumed name.

Many Bretons were punished by 'civil degradation' (stripping them of their citizenship) and some were sentenced to death. One such person was Roparz Hemon. Fortunately for him, a young reporter from the Welsh weekly *Y Faner* attended his trial in Paris in December 1945 – much to the consternation of the French judiciary, who commuted the sentence to imprisonment. The reporter was Dewi

Watkin Powell – now Judge Dewi Watkin Powell – an indefatigable fighter for the Welsh cause ever since. Dewi's report, and the subsequent correspondence in *Y Faner* are a fascinating glimpse of a very testing and nervous time which culminated in a fantastically bold and brave bilingual (Welsh and French) pamphlet published by the Council of the National Eisteddfod – *Adroddiad y ddirprwyaeth i Lydaw Ebrill 1947 (Rapport sur la Visite en Bretagne de la Delegation Galloise, Avril 1947).*

The publication makes a forceful case for the linguistic rights of the Bretons to be respected and for any punishments to be lenient. It also dispelled and challenged the common prejudice of the French psyche against the Breton people and their language in a way not done since Carnhuanawc's highly readable report of his travels to Brittany, which was published in *The Literary Remains of the Rev. Thomas Price, Carnhuanawc* (Llandovery, 1854-55).

Arvel 'slipped under the radar', as Gwenno says, and later found a job at the Plant Breeding Station at Aberystwyth. Thousands of others were not so lucky. Following Dewi Watkin Powell's report, *Y Faner* published a series of letters on the situation in Brittany. These are published in the excellent anthology of Breton literature, The *Turn of the Ermine* by Jacqueline Gibson and Gwyn Griffiths (Francis Boutle Publishers, 2006).

A letter by 'Breton I' estimated that at least 3,000 Bretons were arrested from 1944 onwards and many more were in hiding. The majority of these people, he attested, were not involved in politics. Members of Breton dance and pipe-bands were arrested as were many priests. All Breton papers were banned in August 1944, including the Breton children's magazine *Olole*. Brezoneg er Skol, which provided books for teachers and pupils, was deemed illegal in December 1944 (the chairman, Yann Fouéré, had been thrown into prison in

October 1944), and the teaching of Breton history in primary schools was prohibited. Ropaz Hemon, director of Radio-Roazon, was imprisoned under the incredible charge of 'cultural relations' – which amounted to broadcasting Breton farmers discussing Breton literature. The correspondent listed those who have been executed or condemned to death. As 'Breton II' wrote in *Y Faner*, 23 January 1946, 'Many feel it is the language itself that is on trial'.

It's obvious that the French authorities, with the willing help of pro-France Breton people, saw the capitulation of the Germans as an opportunity to get rid of the Breton movement, or at least to weaken it fatally. The alleged collaboration and treachery (against which country?) was excuse enough for collective punishment of a whole culture. There were neither mass killings nor expulsions, but Breton culture and language became, conveniently, associated with Nazism … a ruse still used by some to this day as a stick to beat down even the most modest of demands for the language. This anti-Breton psychosis seems to ignore the inconvenient fact that millions of French-speakers collaborated with the Nazis, but that their language wasn't attacked. Didn't millions of Germans also collaborate with the Nazis, but was that language discriminated against on German soil?

With the defeat of a vile philosophy based on the concept of *Untermenschen* (sub-humans) the French state slid back to the state philosophy of *Untersprächen* (sub-languages) with ease. And how bad does a state have to be for Nazis, of all people, to make some linguistic concessions to minority languages! The very DNA and philosophy of the French Republic, it seems, breeds an arrogance in many which takes as evident that some languages deserve to die – the Republic of Spite.

However, as we recall in 2009 the anniversary of the beginning of the War, things are changing in Brittany. There is currently a mass campaign to reverse the Nazi decision of splitting Nantes from Brittany, and the culture and language so long ridiculed and humiliated by the French state has refused to die.

Brittany was put in an unenviable situation which we in Wales were thankfully spared. Their choices were how to keep their culture and language alive – decisions which could mean the difference between freedom and imprisonment for men like Arvel or life and death for others. Brittany, like many small nations, chose the wrong (losing) side of the war, crushed between forces stronger than themselves. Maybe, twenty years after other countries have put behind them the defeat of the Second World War, Brittany can do so too. There is certainly a new confidence in Brittany. That is good news for Europe, as the measure of the morality of our continent is how she treats her languages – large and small. Seventy years after the War the innocent Bretons like Arvel Piette, who wanted nothing more than dignity for their language and culture, will be vindicated.

Cambria, volume 11, number 1, June–July 2009

This article caused some reaction from a good friend of mine who is Irish and felt it a slight on her nationality. It wasn't meant as that at all, and nor is it, I believe.

However, I do think it's time for a more honest and balanced view firstly of Irish attitudes towards the Welsh and the Welsh language (attitudes which have not always been positive by a long way) and secondly, by inference, what is the point of Ireland – a country so many Welsh people, including myself, admire.

But I've always been disappointed by most Irish people's lack of knowledge of Wales, and I've always been amazed by the reaction of so many Irish people, through the medium of their articles and letters in the Irish press, to the issue of the Irish language. The Irish state just seems to me to have missed so many opportunities. And the decision to erect a 120 metre needle in O'Connell Street, where the statue of Nelson once stood, just confirmed to me that the state had successfully got rid of one occupier without knowing what to put in its place.

I wrote this article early in 2009, just before the full calamity of the Irish economy became known.

Celtic Cousins?

In the various drunken celebrations of Celtic brotherhood, 'yr hen Wyddeles' is one Welsh idiom you're unlikely to come across. Literally translated, it's 'the old Irishwoman'. However, its meaning and connotations are not that of a homely old Irish grandmother but rather a coarse and scheming woman. I last heard it used by two young men in the gents in a pub in Caernarfon a few years ago discussing a Welsh woman they knew and before that in reference, ironically, to Margaret Thatcher.

So, the relationship between the Welsh and Irish has not always been amicable, as some in mists of Celticism would like us to believe. Suspicion between the two nations stretches back at least as far as Gerald of Wales's writings in the twelfth century. Gerald, part Norman, part Welsh, travelled with the conquering Prince John of England and described the Irish as 'Dedicated only to leisure and laziness, this is a truly barbarous people. They depend on their livelihood for animals and they live like animals' – and that prejudice pretty well sums up the next 800 years for you!

The dogged Catholicism of the Irish for centuries was one central reason for continued suspicion by the Welsh. As the Welsh historian of Irish descent, Paul O'Leary, writes, the relationship came under extra strain when Welsh workers felt that the immigrant Irish were undermining their pay. O'Leary notes that between 1825 and 1882 there were no fewer than twenty anti-Irish riots in Wales, starting with the one in the Rhymni Valley.

The anti-Irish sentiment was given a more cultural context following the publication of the 'Blue Books' in 1847. As O'Leary notes, the effect of the 'treachery' of the Blue Books (the Government's report into education in Wales) was to portray the Welsh as a scheming and immoral nation, with the Welsh language as a medium for that immorality. One Welsh reaction, and the most powerful for generations, was to internalise the colonialism of the Report and also to claim that it wasn't the true Welsh who were to blame. The blame was on those – mostly of the rough industrial regions and non-Chapel goers (read Irish and the anglicised) – who were besmirching Wales's good name. It was 'it isn't us, guv-ism' on a national scale.

However in his excellent article in the Welsh historical journal *Cof Cenedl* XXI of 2006, O'Leary notes a subtle change in the attitudes of some Welsh people from the 1860s. The Monmouthshire columnist 'Gwentwyson' in *Y Cronicl* newspaper of 1863 makes the startling comparison that '*negroaid cathwasiol Lloegr ydy'r Gwyddelod*' (the Irish are the negro slaves of England) and that the Welsh should desist from mocking the Irish as they were the victims of the oppressive policies of Britain in Ireland.

Changes in attitude towards the Irish were given a further boost by the disestablishment of the Anglican Church in Ireland in 1869. This decision raised the possibility that the same could be done in Wales. Despite continued anti-Irish sentiment based on anti-Catholicism and labour issues, parts of the Welsh elite, at least, began to adopt a more appreciative attitude towards the Irish. The great Liberal MP for Meirionnydd, Tom Ellis, supported Irish Home Rule in 1886, and Cymru Fydd (Young Wales) was inspired by the Irish model. Patrick Pearse himself, one of the instigators of the 1916 Rebellion, was accepted into the Gorsedd of the Bards at the National Eisteddfod at Cardiff in 1899, and the success of Sinn Féin's rebellion was a direct influence on the founders of Plaid Cymru, which became a party of government in the National Assembly in 2007.

But however little is understood of the Irish in Wales and the attitude of the Welsh to the Irish, even less is written on the attitudes of the Irish to the Welsh – in Wales or Ireland. For the history of the Irish in Wales is a complex one, the added twist being that however lowly the Irish were, unlike the native Welsh, they still possessed and spoke the imperial language, English. This created a paradoxical situation of a weak social community speaking the prestigious powerful state language, English, as opposed to a relatively stronger social community speaking a weaker, less prestigious language, Welsh. This situation led to instances of Irish prejudice against Welsh, which is rarely mentioned in polite political circles in Ireland, and never discussed in Irish academic articles.

I'd contend that there's an untold story of Irish prejudice

towards the Welsh and especially towards the Welsh language. On purely anecdotal evidence it seems to me that the Irish as a community in Wales have adopted in the past, rather paradoxically, an Ulster Unionist-type attitude towards the Welsh language.

Until the last few generations or so, efforts which we would today call 'integration' of the Irish community by the Welsh were rarely successful. The Irish were separated from the Welsh working class by their lack of knowledge of Welsh and their Catholicism. Preachers like Ieuan Gwynedd, who succeeded in attracting Irish children from the streets of Tredegar in the 1840s to attend Welsh Sunday Schools, were few in number. The Irish became, ironically, a force for the Anglicisation of Welsh society. The Irish, as a community, started to become integrated only when the native Welsh became anglicised. Although data is not available, I'd be surprised if, despite support for Mother Ireland and Irish emancipation among the Irish communities of Wales, as a community, that support extended to supporting Welsh home rule until very recently … and maybe not even during the 1997 referendum. Politically, linguistically and culturally, the working-class Irish communities in Wales have been bastions of English-language culture and upholders of the structures of the British state. The biggest cultural effect of the Irish as a community in Wales has been to make Wales an English-speaking country.

If the Irish have suffered prejudice at the hands of the Welsh, the Welsh have suffered from ignorance at the hands of the Irish. Many Irish still habitually refer to landing in Holyhead or Fishguard as landing in England. Speaking Welsh can be mocked and insulted as much by Irish people as by our other neighbours. Irish knowledge of Wales, from my experience, rarely reaches the dizzy heights of even the common English clichés. Numerous visits to Ireland have led me to expect a blank look as I explain I'm from Wales and they desperately search for a polite answer or cultural reference. Conversations which do commence on the theme seem pre-programmed by Bord Fáilte day courses in hospitality – one-sided conversations where I yearn for the honesty of silence.

Whilst the Irish think of Wales (if they think of Wales at all) as an extension of England, most Welsh people, even today after the Troubles and eighty years of independence, think of Ireland as being just a slightly errant part of the UK. Independent yes, but really, you know, they're a part of Britain ... maybe they're both right.

The more politically-minded Irish are possibly baffled by Welsh subservience whilst the Irish attitude towards the Irish language is a source of amazement to the nationalist Welsh. How is it, the Welsh think, that a nation surrounded by a sea, which has seen no immigration for 400 years, can so completely lose their language? How is it I can nonchalantly be served in Welsh in a garage 100 miles from the metropolis of Liverpool or Manchester but not be served in Irish 300 miles further west?

So, Ireland, as well as a source of inspiration to generations of Welsh nationalists since the days of Emrys ap Iwan in the late nineteenth century, also serves as a warning. Saunders Lewis, a big Hibernophile, warned, with a knowing look towards Ireland, that winning independence before winning the language would be fatal to Welsh. With the exception of the brave first live broadcasts in Welsh coming from Dublin rather than Wales in the 1920s, Irish moral support for Wales or the Welsh language has been notable by its absence. The introduction of the *Gaeltacht* (areas in Ireland 'reserved' for speakers of Irish) in the 1950s had some influence on the Adfer movement and the concept of the Fro Gymraeg, but that's about it.

But then maybe Ireland's biggest gift to Wales has been to be there – and to be independent.

For, despite this history, there is so much to celebrate and inspire in Wales' relationship with Ireland. Of the half a dozen Irish people I know well, all are Welsh-speaking and my life is richer for knowing them. Although the present-day politics of the Republic seem at times to be a rainier and bigger version of Ceredigion, the Irish Risorgimento of the late nineteenth and early twentieth century still inspires thousands of Welsh people, including myself. Ireland offers an alternative, that of a state whose own self-worth isn't of a desperate mutton-dressed-as-lamb ex-super-power trying to strut her stuff on the world stage. Its army 'serves neither King nor Kaiser but Ireland'.

But Ireland's strength is the elixir it refuses to drink. A leader of smaller nations, a battler for the underdog? It timidly skulks away. It could have spoken up in Europe during the negotiations on the Nice Treaty for the right of nations like the Catalans and Basques to choose their constitutional future, as outlined in the Good Friday Agreement for the Irish. (This is a right that is illegal under the Spanish constitution.) But it didn't. It could use its veto to demand that France sign the Charter on Minority Languages and so recognise the right of their fellow Celtic language, Breton, to live. But it won't.

Which begs the question, 'What's the point of Ireland?' Why, in a post-Catholic, post-Republican and possible post-Irish-language state, *have* an Irish state? Is it enough to say, 'because we feel Irish' or 'because we don't want change'? Certainly peace for over eighty years in the Republic is a good answer. But, should there be more than that? It's not that I believe that Ireland should rejoin the UK – far from it. But I know the moral reason for a Welsh state – to defend and promote the Welsh language; I'm not so sure today of the moral reason for an Irish one? Or am I guilty of defining Irish nationality by Welsh standards, and of ignorance of Ireland?

Maybe the journey to independence, or the cultural movement that goes with it, is the exciting part. Maybe, the journey is more important than the destination. If so, is Wales not the new Ireland? Are we in Wales, all of us, now, where the Irish were in the late nineteenth and early twentieth century? And if so, can we have an honest appraisal of the relationship between our two nations as we, too, become a nation-state?

If we're ready to abandon the 'hen Wyddeles' and the other old prejudices on both sides, then the road to statehood for Wales, like Ireland before her, is the right road.

Cambria, volume 10, number 6, March-April 2009

My father's family are originally from Brecon. During the 1960s both his parents and his two sisters found work in Swansea (Abertawe), settling in Llansamlet, a big new housing estate to the east of the city. Every month we would drive to Swansea in our Vauxhall Victor (and later in the Lada) to see my grandparents, Alice and Stanley Jobbins. We'd always be served a marvellous Sunday lunch with fruit tart and custard and then a little bar of Milky Way chocolate to enjoy on the long journey home to Cardiff on the A40.

Later, sitting as the student union representative on West Glamorgan County Council's Education committee in 1989–90 I had a lesson in the pettiness of class jingoism and institutional anti-Welsh sentiment. Here were the councillors who managed, through their wilful ignorance, to take the spiv end of capitalism and marry it with the latest socialist rhetoric of anti-individual, big state brutalism. They thus justified demolishing the once beautiful city of Swansea, creating instead one even the Soviets would be embarrassed by.

What the local council have done to Swansea is a tragedy, and they have denied Wales a second city worthy of the name.

Swansea – Where's That?

If I say 'Paris', what comes to mind? Undoubtedly an image of the Eiffel Tower or Notre Dame. Likewise, closer to home, Cardiff brings to mind the Civic Centre or the Millennium Stadium and possibly the new Assembly building. Smaller towns in Wales can also paint a picture in your mind: Caernarfon, Aberystwyth, even Port Talbot; but what of our second city, Swansea? For those who don't live in the city, does Swansea create any picture at all? If not, is that the fault of the city itself, or is it the fault of the media?

Dylan Thomas may come to mind, but then it's as a poet

who came from the town, not one who encapsulated it in verse. His most famous work, *Under Milk Wood*, was inspired by New Quay, fifty miles to the west. I guess many of my readers would be hard pushed to have a clear image of what the city actually looks like. Dylan's 'pretty ugly city' seems more of a 'pretty unknown city'. This all says much about Wales' second city, and Wales' media.

Since devolution, a trickle of national institutions have come to Swansea but this hardly amounts to Corporate Wales' whole-hearted anointing of the place as our Second City. One such institution was the National Swimming Centre; was this some kind of patronising Cardiff joke to keep the Swansea Jacks happy, perhaps? The latest arrival is the National Waterfront Museum. One only hopes it can be more successful and loved in Swansea than it was when it was based in a wet and windy dockside in Cardiff. The closure, dismantling and subsequent relocation of this museum to Swansea barely raised a whimper in the capital. No matter how interesting a collection might be, that's what happens when penny-pinching, populist politicians locate it in a building so mediocre that nobody cares if it is bulldozed. Had a building of the National Museum's elegance been moved to Swansea, my guess is that there would have been an outrage from *South Wales Echo* readers (the most influential people in Labour's Wales). Here's a lesson to Assembly Members and local town planners: nobody remembers the price of a building, only its worth.

Wales, like Scotland, Denmark or Croatia, is one of Europe's three- or four-city countries. In the topsy-turvy world of Welsh-speaking Wales, there are three cities: Caerdydd (Cardiff), Aberystwyth and what could be called Dinas Menai – the conurbation of Bangor and Porthaethwy down to Caernarfon and its old slate-quarrying hinterland. Swansea, a city of 200,000, barely touches the Welsh-language radar screen, even though 10 per cent of the county's population – some 25,000 people – are Welsh-speaking. The city's Welsh-language contribution today is but a hamlet of activity and pales into insignificance against such metropolises of *cynghanedd*, choirs and pop-groups as small towns like Porthmadog or Bala.

But what of the mental topography of English-speaking Wales? I'm increasingly unsure whether Swansea is our second city in any meaningful way here either. In fact, I suspect that in the medium of English, Wales is in danger of becoming a one-city state.

There is much competition, if not animosity, between Cardiff and Swansea, but do the two vie with each other in the intellectual and cultural spheres? Welsh-speakers in Cardiff will discuss what's going on in Caernarfon or Aberystwyth. These centres have their own cultural agendas and each speaks out with a distinct voice. But I've never heard anyone in Cardiff discuss 'Swansea' as a distinct cultural package. Cardiffians talk in shorthand of 'The Valleys' or North Wales' or even 'West Wales' (wherever that starts) as distinct cultural geographies, and they may bracket the second city under the first or the third. What they never do is talk of 'Swansea' as shorthand for a distinct cultural force itself in national life.

It may be that this says more about Cardiff than Swansea. It certainly says much about our media and where the power and gravity of our media lies. But that a city can be ignored, and allow itself to be ignored, says volumes about the city itself. Swansea's history is one of useless civic leaders too petty-minded to see the big picture and always able to miss opportunities.

Things could have turned out very differently. There are two interesting books yet to be written about Wales. One is about the most important underlying feature of Welsh political life, *The History of Apathy in Wales* (if any historian could be bothered to write it). The other book is *What if?'* of Welsh history. In moments of idle thought I indulge in the 'what ifs' of our history.

One great 'what if' concerns the attempted invasion by French republican forces at Carreg Wastad near Fishguard in 1797 – what is touristically called the Last Invasion (as if the massive movement of English-speakers into Wales which has changed the language and culture of our country since then isn't an invasion).

What if the French had been successful and we had been liberated? As the biggest town in Wales with some 7,000 people, its mercantile class and location, what if it had been proclaimed the capital of a Cambrian Republic, in the way that Laibach, now Ljubljana, became capital of the Illyrian Provinces in its short eight years under Napoleon's occupation from 1808–1816 – an occupation which changed Slovene culture, language and politics for ever?

Would Swansea have drawn Iolo Morganwg, Ywain Myfyr, Morris Morris and the other dreamers and poets of the early nineteenth century to its cobbled streets, creating the first Welsh city? Would it have given Welsh the status it deserved and raised the possibility of Wales being a country in its own right with its own parliament – a thought which never seemed even to enter the minds of the Welsh, not even of Iolo, until the late nineteenth century? Could Swansea as capital of a Cambrian Republic have punctured the nascent Methodist Revival?

Then, the town was home to industrious and cultured people. The Dillwyn Llewellyn family of Penlle'rgaer, within the present city boundaries, were at the forefront of photography. The oldest photo taken in Wales was a Daguerrotype of Margam Castle in 1841, and one of the world's earliest albums of photographs was created by a woman, Mary Dillwyn, in the Swansea area. Wales's first modern newspaper, *The Cambrian*, was published in Swansea in 1804. Had the town elders held more vision, Swansea's new library built in 1860s could have been Wales's national library. In fact, had the national revival began in Wales in earnest a generation earlier, as it had done in other stateless nations in Eastern Europe, then Swansea, as the most dynamic town of the first half of the nineteenth century, with its middle class and population may have become our capital.

But that wasn't to be. Swansea closed in on itself, became ever more suspicious of the Welsh-speaking hill-dwellers who had the town surrounded, viewing them with a contempt near to racism.

Swansea is a fascinating border town. The western city's dipping cymoedd create a true sense of interconnecting villages drawn together by the magnificent, shapely sweep of Swansea Bay. Yet until this very last generation the strength of the Welsh language, always but a village away from Swansea, has created a great suspicion amongst the town's dwellers. To become a true Jack was to deny the Welsh language, if not to yourself, then to your children. Dylan Thomas, born to a Welsh-speaking family, is the most famous, but not only, example. If Dylan had been brought up speaking and writing in Welsh, would he today be so well-known? Perhaps not outside Wales, but perhaps his contribution to Wales' own internal life would have been immeasurably more constructive. What if Gwenallt, the communist-cum-Christian, had been born and brought up in Abertawe rather than Cwm Tawe? What would his poetry be, and in which language?

There is something beguiling about the two-handed Jack, one set of knuckles tattooed with the word 'hate', the other with 'love'. Swansea's peeling streets seem unloved even by its own people. Its evening paper, the *Evening Post*, seems poorer than Cardiff's *Echo*. Rare are the poets and singers who sing the city's praise, yet there are real ingredients here for something more. This is a city where the locals look you in the eye and still say 'hello' rather than stare self-consciously at the pavement or look away. The Christian composer, Mal Pope, sings a lonely song for his home town; the folk group Boys From the Hill strive to create an urban folk culture reminiscent of Dublin's sprawling estates, where Townhill becomes Tallaght. In Welsh, Neil Rosser's *Nos Sadwrn Abertawe* is a rousing elegy to the Hoggarthian Saturday night at the boozy, brawling Kingsway. Huw Chiswell, a native of the Tawe Valley, casts a sentimental but honest eye at metropolitan Swansea, the city from the Llwchwr to the Afan. It was Swansea historians, with the late Glanmor Williams at their head, who resuscitated the study of Welsh history in the 1970s. So, why is it that the whole seems less than the sum of its parts?

Are, then, the politicians to blame? Is it that the local council has been run for generations by councillors trapped in their boorish class jingoism, councillors with the inane self-satisfaction which only the stupid can acquire? Is it that the undercurrent of anti-Welshness, always an element in British Labour, has mitigated against having a frank and mature discussion about 'what is Wales, and what is the point of its second city now that nobody wants her coal and copper'?

What is it about Swansea which makes it so invisible to the media? How can BBC Wales never think of it as a city? It's like one of those secret Soviet cities which were never located on the map. Why has it never been the location of a soap-opera or detective series? With the exception of the incongruous Proms concert televised every September from Singleton Park, when Knightsbridge comes to the Mumbles, it's a job to recall the last time the city was on TV. Why, the BBC even closed down its studio at the graceful Glyn Vivian Gallery! S4C's nightly *Heno* programme was broadcast from the city, but now goes out from the more glamorous location of a carbuncle in Llanelli. How unattractive does a place have to be to be upstaged by a Llanelli multi-storey car park?

Is it that Swansea is not far enough away from Cardiff? Is it now merely Cardiff's furthest western suburb? In twenty-first century UK Swansea is still a surprisingly white city. Does that not make it interesting and diverse enough for the attentions of the mediacrats? Maybe it's not gritty enough to be 'proper Valleys' or rural enough to appeal to the white flight generation. Is architecture the problem, with Swansea's misfortune that it was blitzed in the 1940s only to be reconstructed with the charm of East European Communism?

Whatever the causes, it's a crying shame for, as I hint, it seems to me that Swansea is so much more interesting than Cardiff, with its petty bourgeoisie and smugocracy. Wales needs a strong, Welsh, Swansea. Wales needs a 'Swansea' that has a much more defined cultural identity, recognised and reacted to throughout the land. Swansea also has to ask what it is for, to engage with Wales and not be afraid of it. Maybe, in that respect, the Welsh media, singers, playwrights and poets have a practical part to play. Who knows, it may even make for good viewing.

Cambria, volume 7, number 5, November–December 2005

With the exception of meetings in London or catching flights from English airports I rarely go to England any more, which is a pity and something I'm determined to change. When I do, I find myself instinctively looking for the Welsh version of the road sign or railway timetable!

There has been some talk since the mid 1990s of a growing 'English' awareness (distinct from 'Britishness'). This to me seems a more honest identity and something I'm glad to see. Since the late Middle Ages, at least, those who've wished to frustrate Welsh linguistic, cultural and political aspirations have done so in the name of Britain rather than of England. Wales's 'problem' isn't England, it's 'Britain'.

England am byth!

England and the Scandinavianisation of Britain

I had a novel experience watching the 2007 Rugby World Cup. For the first time ever I wasn't supporting ATBE (Any Team But England). Whilst I didn't rush out to buy a plastic Cross of Saint George flag, I'd go as far as saying that I would have been quite glad had the English retained the Webb Ellis Trophy.

I've traditionally taken the ATBE position not through anti-English xenophobia, but for political reasons. Were I, and thousands of other Welsh people to support England, the media and political class wouldn't applaud us for our cultural generosity but would see the equation: the Welsh support England, ergo, the Welsh are essentially English. Not supporting England is an easy-to-read way of making the point: 'we're Welsh, don't take us for granted'.

Which brings me back to my surprising Damascene revelation. My relaxed attitude towards English success at this exciting World Cup of underdogs had nothing to do with a newfound feeling of Brownite Great-British nationalism, and nor am I comfortable with English flags flying in Wales. After all, the first recorded use of the St George's Cross as an emblem of England was in a Roll of Accounts relating to Edward I's war of 1275 against Welsh independence – his *Drang nach Westen*. How would the Poles feel seeing the Teutonic flag fluttering over the rooftops of Warsaw? English flags flying in Aberystwyth are a sign of an English cultural, linguistic and economic power dwarfing a weak Welsh identity – it's like Edward's army is back in town.

But I do enjoy bittersweet irony. The success of the England rugby team (and my support for that success), far from strengthening the Great British narrative, undermines it. With every drop-goal Jonny Wilkinson kicked in France the ties of Britishness weakened and Englishness strengthened a little. Put simply, the stronger English sentiment becomes, the stronger becomes the call for an English parliament and with that, by implication, a stronger Welsh parliament. Since I believe that the moral purpose of creating Welsh nationality is to be a vehicle to strengthen the Welsh language and culture, and since those most hostile to the Welsh language and Welsh nationality are the ones most keen to promote Britishness, then a specifically increasing *English* awareness is good news. That's why I find myself able to support the *English* rugby team but not a *British* athletics team. Britishness claims territorial jurisdiction over Welsh culture and political aspiration, Englishness doesn't.

The rise in English self-awareness is now well-documented. However, what's interesting from a Welsh point of view is the difference between 'English nationalism' and the Welsh version. Whilst Welsh nationalism is very much part of the left-wing, idealistic epoch of the civil rights and anti-colonial movements of the 1960s, 'English nationalism' is of today. It's a more right-of-centre, cynical (or realistic – if you like) zeitgeist rooted in the politics of the new century – democracy and demography.

In his excellent book on the political philosophy of Plaid Cymru, *Rhoi Cymru'n Gyntaf* (University of Wales Press) Dr Richard Wyn Jones draws our attention to the three steps of nationalist development identified by the Czech historian, Miroslav Hroch. Step A is the intellectual activity which gives the national community its self-awareness, by studying and elevating that community's language, culture and history. In the Welsh case this would be represented by the era of Iolo Morganwg. Step B develops from the work of pioneers – a concerted effort to spread the national awareness among the general population. Again, the Welsh version is represented by people like Michael D. Jones, the minister who founded the Welsh-speaking community in Patagonia, or Emrys ap Iwan, a gardener's son from Abergele, who became a linguist, but strongly opposed the building of English-language chapels in Welsh-speaking areas. The final step, Step C, sees a critical mass of the population accepting the importance of their 'new-found' national identity, at which point it becomes a hegemonic force, penetrating all walks of the nation's life from trade unionism to education and commerce. This final step didn't happen fully in Wales, or at least it hasn't happened yet.

From a Welsh point of view, what is interesting about English nationalism is the absence of the Step A group of people. Who is the English Iolo Morganwg, Slovak Streymeyer or Slovene Prešeren? In fact, who are the intellectuals championing English nationalism? It seems to have gone in one leap straight to Step B, if not Step C. Of course, the English have never had to validate nor justify their language or culture – it's never been banned or been under threat. England didn't have such a 'peasant culture' as we Welsh or, say, the Estonians had. And yet, as this new

English nationalism recreates a new political English identity, one would expect to see English intellectuals giving it a voice. But more of this later.

And what of Step B, the acceptance of this new identity being broadcast by a second generation of nationalists: Michael D. Jones in Wales, L'udovít Stúr in Slovakia, Josip Juraj Strossmayer in Croatia and Frantisek Palacky for the Czechs? Again, the English link is weak. It seems there are no nationally-known leaders fighting the case for English nationalism – or is it that they're yet to become well-known? And this may be the biggest difference between the English and Welsh or other 'non-historic nations'.

Whilst Welsh and East European nineteenth-century nationalism was stuffed full of ministers, sons of ministers, teachers and publishers, English nationalism seems to have totally by-passed this class of people. English nationalism, so different from Welsh nationalism, is the nationalism of the self-made man, the White Van Man. A man caricatured for his lack of fine words and concepts.

English nationalism doesn't bribe intellectuals with quotes by Italian Marxist nor French philosophers. Indeed, it's too uncouth for some. English nationalism is part of the belief system of the self-made man who owes nothing to anyone, whose occupation doesn't depend on 'Britain' – unlike British politicians, the British media who need to sustain a British context for their work, the British industrialists of the large retail stores or trade unions. Nor does English nationalism depend on the traditional working-class occupations which upheld Britishness – such as coal-mining or ship-building. They are long gone. The White Van Man of English nationalism doesn't need Britishness. His economic sphere is his local market town or conurbation. Britain is either too big or, in the globalised economy with China and India, too small.

Yet despite this seeming classical absence of Steps A and B, English nationalism is starting to develop a hold on English aspiration, undermining Britishness from within. How is this happening? Well an obvious answer is that English nationalism is strengthened by its uneasy tango with Celtic nationalism. Again, the phenomenal (and, yes, lucky) success of Celtic nationalism in 2007 is something whose consequences are yet to be fully felt. The July 2007 meeting of the Council of Isles seemed as if *Armes Prydain*, the tenth-century Welsh prophesy of the Bretons, Irish, Manx, Scots and Welsh uniting against the English, seemed to have become fulfilled on the windy steps of Stormont – yet in this setting the English weren't the 'enemy', since they didn't have their own spokesperson. There were Alex Salmond of Scotland, Gerry Adams and Bertie Ahern of Ireland, and Ieuan Wyn Jones of Wales, but it was the Scot, Gordon Brown, the flag-waver of a born-again 'British nationalism', who represented England. 'Britishness', like Welshness and Englishness, is a political choice rather than an ethnic identity.

Incredibly, 'British nationalists' attack English nationalists for promoting an ethnic English identity. This flies in the face of reason, as the calls to create an English parliament, will, by definition, create a new England polity and civic identity – incidentally, a cause championed by another Scot, Sir Malcolm Rifkind. And if some members of the ethnic minority feel cold towards Englishness, should not the organs of the state now be promoting an 'inclusive' Englishness rather than flogging the (dead?) horse of 'Britishness', which seems in danger of being the minority identity of choice of white English people? As Richard Wyn Jones also makes clear, we're all nationalists, whether as part of the various strands of the 'banal nationalism' of the dominant state which Gordon Brown's party so wholeheartedly supports, or the aspiring, forward-looking nationalism of the Welsh, the English, the Scots or the Cornish. Those of the 'British nationalist' variety in government or opposition have no reason to look down their noses at Celtic or, indeed, English nationalists – the concept of Britishness has plenty of blood on its hands. Those who claim not to be nationalists at all share the same conceit as those red-neck American whites who claimed that only other people were 'of colour'.

The attack on the supposed danger of English nationalism, and on calls for an English Parliament, draws parallels with Neil Kinnock's opposition to the Welsh Assembly in 1979. Richard Wyn Jones (his book is currently being translated into English) recalls how Kinnock argued that Welsh nationality should continue to be a 'matter of hearts and minds, not of bricks, committees and bureaucrats'. That is, although Kinnock had no opposition to the continuance of Welshness in its ethnic form (if we put the question of the Welsh language to one side) he didn't support giving civic expression to that Welshness. By opposing an English parliament, aren't Brown's 'British nationalists' just as guilty of confining English identity to the ethnic rather than the civic?

Britishness seemed once so strong and may be so again, but from the standpoint of the England-supporting rugby and football fan it's looking increasingly irrelevant. Funnily enough, the traits which made Welshness seem so weak now seem to be its strength – which may have some bearing on Englishness too.

When Britishness was at its height in the nineteenth century, Welsh identity and language seemed equated with femininity (should I say with the contemporary implication of weakness?) – the cartoon figure of 'Dame Wales', *mamwlad* (motherland), *mamiaith* (mother tongue). Welsh was the language of the *'gegin gefn'* (the back kitchen), it was the language of the hearth, not the office. Isn't it indicative of this that the branches of the Urdd, the Welsh-language youth movement, are called *'aelwyd'* (hearth)? When Welsh was allowed in school it was reserved for the female-dominated primary schools. And when it was eventually taught in high schools, Welsh tended to be the language of the more 'feminine' social sciences. Britishness, with its English language, in comparison, was a real man's world. English, like British identity, was associated with the science, war and finance.

But, it seems, the tortoise of 'feminine' Welsh identity was able to overtake the testosterone-fuelled hare of Britishness. Maybe, with the 'feminisation' of society, such male virtues are not so important. Maybe in the age of 'identity politics' people naturally feel greater affinity and love for their mothers' side. Is this true in England too? As the old nation-states of the nineteenth century lose much of their power to global finance, Britain doesn't seem so practical, what now is the point of Britain? Does the City of London, for instance, that bastion of British commerce, now need Britain? Would an English parliament really damage the City of London? With the Bank of England now independent, would it really care if England itself was independent too? With the exception of fighting wars, what can Britain do which England (or Wales) can't?

So, who are the new English pioneers, the Iolo Morganwgs of the English cause? If it was the ragged, exotic antiquarians who revived or invented Welsh, Estonian or Slovene identity in the nineteenth century, my guess is that it could be historians in the twenty-first century. There's a newfound interest in English history. Not a slip-of-the-tongue England-when-we-mean-Britain, but *England*. It's a historic step in English historiography which puts a full-stop to the arrogance which started in the tenth century when Ealdorman Aethelweard declared that Britain 'is now called England, thereby assuming the name of the victor'.

Of course, this doesn't discount the need to create a multi-ethnic English identity – and I don't think it will. If nations are 'invented communities', as our intellectual class have told us over the past twenty years, then all communities can be re-invented. And if a boil-in-the-bag African state like Zambia, my country of birth, created from nothing in 1911 and gaining independence in 1966, can create a national narrative, then surely it's not beyond the wit of the English to create a national narrative which can, and does, include people of different races and backgrounds.

Political Britishness is being challenged. Britain's main supporters seem now to be the incongruous extremes of the BNP and the CRE. A while ago the Conservative party suggested setting up an English Grand Committee. My guess is that the Tories know this isn't workable, and the Grand Committee is a bit of kite-flying to check that the wind's blowing favourably before they go for a proper English parliament. But would a stronger English identity be so threatening?

Were England to have her own Parliament, even in the unlikely situation of the break-up of the UK, would that really mean the 'Balkanisation of Britain' as Pontpridd MP Kim Howells so graphically warned us in true camp, British, *Hammer-House-of-Horror* style? No, of course not. It would be less 'Balkanisation', more 'Scandinavianisation'. It may not be as snappy a term, with too many syllables, but it's a far more appropriate political analogy, representing, as it does, three closely-related nation-states, cooperating to their mutual economic and cultural benefit, but taking their own decisions. In fact it would be a bargain – three states for the price of one. As we celebrate cultural diversity should we not now also celebrate constitutional diversity too? Britain would still exist, but would not three nation-states on the island give us true diversity and choice – or does diversity stop at food and music? And we already have several examples of real living Scandinavianisation of Britain: the Anglican church, the rugby, football, boxing or bowling unions; the legal deposit libraries;and, in politics, education and health policies. And talking of politics, when will the media and the government realise that the parliament in Westminster is increasingly, in everything but name, an English parliament? The Health, Education and Transport Secretaries are de facto English ministers, as the remit of Westminster doesn't run the other side of Offa's Dyke or Hadrian's Wall.

So who will decide to ride the English lion out of the current union, as Boris Yeltsin did with Russia in the USSR and Vaclav Klaus with the Czech republic and Czechoslovakia? To go back to Hroch's three steps, the first two were there already, albeit perhaps being re-written, but it is the last step which is missing. It's too early yet, but politics and culture are changing fast and when the English begin to mean England and not Britain when they say 'in this country', then the British flag will be a limp one. Who then wouldn't bet that one politician might not go for glory and close the circle of English history-making as Europe's earliest nation-states becomes the continent's newest?

Cambria, volume 9, number 4, November–December 2007

Real living Welshness

It seems that cycles of nostalgia in pop music and fashion follows a twenty-year rotation. So, by the mid 2000s, it was time to revive the 1980s.

With the third Assembly election on the horizon in May 2007, Wales and Britain grabbing oxygen masks as the property price boom reached new altitudes of eye watering prices, and the UK in two foreign wars, there was for me something irritating, to say the least, with the newly-found nostalgia for the 1980s, a decade whose music and fashion were now becoming ironically trendy. What was worse was that those who'd shouted the 'Maggie, Maggie, Maggie - out out out!' slogans of the decade were now in power and implementing her economic policies.

A few weeks after this article was published in Cambria *magazine, Labour lost several seats at the Assembly elections and then the UK economic boom became the economic bust. It will take years for the UK to get over the excess of property prices, state-sponsored population change and 'hitting above our weight' – if ever. It was also the high tide of the narrative of 'progressive politics' and of 'rights of man' begun by Voltaire and Rousseau. The future will be conservative.*

Don't mention the 1980s

Just a thought: can I sue a decade? C'mon, my readership must include some lawyers who want a break from profiting from other people's bad judgement and bad luck. How about this for a case? The media is full of 1980s retrospectives at the moment, and the politicians and programme-makers are people whose formative years were the 80s, but I'd like to sue the 1980s for being such a terrible decade and for casting an unwarranted shadow on Welsh political life – for all the wrong reasons.

My eighties-phobia re-emerged, like a particularly bad

curry, as I drove down to Cardiff in the winter of 2006. Real Radio, the commercial station for southern Wales, had an 'Eighties Anthems' show on, celebrating all those 'hair spray' rock songs of my youth. My stomach turned all the way from Carmarthen to the Capital, a nervousness filling my vitals as reminders of past uncertainties and teenage awkwardness churned my belly. Maybe more than any other decade, there were two sides to the 1980s – one, the 80s of the Yuppies, Falklands War, Thatcherism and Wham!, and then there was the other, the alternative 80s of CND, soggy protest marches, the Miners' Strike and The Smiths. Yeah, and guess which 1980s I was a part of! Now, don't get me wrong, I graduated in 1989, and I did have a good time in the eighties, but apart from the Welsh-language rock scene, I have no nostalgia for the decade at all, only regret and anger. It's been and it's over so why couldn't the media just leave it at that?

Unfortunately, it seemed the media just wouldn't leave it – it was that feeling of deja vu all over again. Women's magazines were full of features on retro 1980s fashion which seems to mean the return of the dreaded leggings: those awful, bum-sagging, knee-indented, shapeless trousers. I spent the 1980s wishing women would dress, well . . . like women. Instead it was the decade when feminists decided not to look feminine and wore Doc Marten boots, leggings and horrible floral skirts. Radio Cymru was also in on the act, broadcasting a turgid *hiraethothon* every Saturday morning, playing all the worst songs of the 1980s. This totally uncalled-for provocation invited me to bark at the radio like a madman, much to the bemusement of Owain, my one-year old son.

But back to my salmonella, re-heated, 80s moment on the M4. Somewhere before Pyle, where the Margam Steelworks rises like Tel Aviv from the sand dunes, an unfamiliar sound crept out of Real Radio. It was the thud of the shoulder pads against the soft mutation which confirmed just how much we've (thankfully) moved on since that decade. The strangely unfamiliar and yet so very familiar sound seeping from the Real Radio 80sfest was nothing less than the sound of the Welsh language. It was in the form of an advert in Welsh promoting the Assembly Government's health campaign to raise awareness of back-pain (Real Radio listeners being prime candidates for 'sickie-taking', it would seem). The advert was in Welsh promoting the stupendously-named website www.cefnaucymru.com. Hallelujah for back-pain! So unfamiliar and out of context was it, that I was almost embarrassed at not recognising my own language. But, hearing an advert in Welsh on an English-language radio station put there by the National Assembly Government is something which wouldn't have, couldn't have happened in the 1980s. That's one other good reason for not having any nostalgia for that dreadful decade, and why it should be binned rather than recycled.

Some things, then, have changed a lot since the 1980s. Others haven't. The Conservatives under that nice Mr Cameron have started to apologise for their mistakes in the eighties. The politics of apology is a sorry state of affairs, but now that the Conservatives are reassessing their contribution to the 1980s, isn't it also time others in Wales reassess what lessons we should take from that decade?

In Welsh mythology the 1980s were, in the words of the great historian Gwyn Alf Williams, 'the years of the plague'. That may be largely true, but is it the whole story, and are the Tories the only ones who should repent and admit their mistakes?

I was at a book launch recently held by anti-nuclear campaigners who claimed that their sit-ins around Greenham Common helped end the Cold War. Really? That would be news to the Soviets, who were brought to their knees economically by the nuclear arms race, but brought to their knees laughing by CND's rainbow scarves and mittens. Nothing I have ever read suggests that the anti-nuclear campaign did anything to bring the arms race to an end. It's pure self-delusion, and a collective self-delusion which goes unchallenged by many in Wales.

Likewise, the Tories are blamed for the closure of the coalmines. I remember collecting food outside Asda in Whitchurch, Cardiff, for the families of the strikers, but does anyone believe there would be many more mines left here today had Thatcher not been in power?

Thatcher, the Ugly Sister forever 'behind us' in the pantomime of Welsh politics did the 'dirty work' which left-wing politicians can boo-hiss her for. They're the same MPs and AMs who are eternally grateful that she was man enough to save them from taking tough decisions. Are these the same left-wing politicians and journalists who celebrate or who work in the information economy of Cŵl Cymru? The UK's service and creative industries were built on the realisation that UK manufacturing could not compete with cheaper economies – a realism many chose to ignore in the 1980s, but which they now scoff from the trough of IT and the media.

As this column originally went to print the elections for the third Assembly were in full swing. And what a bizarre election it was for an Assembly which seemed not to touch people's lives one iota for 200 weeks until the convenient smoking ban and free prescriptions of the last week of its mandate.

As ever, Labour's increasingly Völkish iconisation of the Valleys' communities was in evidence. Its iconisation wouldn't have been out of place in those East European socialist workers' posters of kerchiefed women and muscular men, or even a nineteenth-century Welsh-language novel.

Like Fianna Fàil's republican narrative in Ireland, it's a narrative which is rooted more in myth than reality. As with Fianna Fàil, the politics of the 1930s is continuously being refought. First there was the Strike of 1984 and then the closure of the Burberry factory in 2006: the latest in a line of misfortune from which the Rhondda, more than anywhere else perhaps, should have been saved.

There is something profoundly rotten about Welsh politics and especially about the political class, now in their 40s and 50s, who were active in the 1980s. The visceral anti-Thatcher hostility – almost a sort of 'anti-Tory racism', which is invoked right across the political spectrum, contributes nothing whatsoever to our political debate.

If some Conservatives are mature enough to admit to the mistakes of the 1980s isn't it time for their adversaries to do so too? I don't mean apologising for slavery or the Holocaust and other events which left-wing MPs personally had nothing to do with – that's easy – it's just showing off. No; I mean apologising for things which Welsh politicians did in Wales.

Rather than keeping up the anti-Tory rhetoric at the same time as implementing Tory policy, isn't it time for politicians and political activists to come clean and say they got things wrong? We could have a mass Peace-and-Reconciliation-type event, as they had in South Africa, with politicians broadcasting live apologies on S4C and BBC2 Wales. What about, for instance: opposing 'Thatcherite' economic policies in the 1980s yet implementing the very same in the 2000s; apologising for hounding Welsh-speakers as racists in 2001 for voicing concern over the ability of Welsh-speaking Wales to integrate English-speakers, whilst implementing policies to integrate newcomers in English a year later; or apologising for opposing nuclear power in the 1980s but supporting it in 2007; or saying sorry to Norman Tebbitt for ridiculing his 'cricket test' in 1992, but proposing a 'British test' in 2006. We could go on and on ...

Of course, 'we're all Thatcherites' now. Or rather the electorate is. They, we, us, don't say that, of course. When the cold wind of capitalism threatens your job, then everyone's a socialist. Not so much Stalin's 'communism in one country' nor Trotsky's 'world-wide communism', but more 'communism in one person'; a nimbyism of the jobs market, if you like. Obviously nobody's honest enough to say this. So, when Burberry closed its factory in the Rhondda in 2007 we got out the old 'socialist' campaign flags. Labour politicians were incapable of campaigning with any intellectual integrity against the closure as they'd just signed a treaty with China to broaden Free Trade (of which Burberry took full advantage and moved its production to a union-free factory in the People's Republic). So Labour, having lost the intellectual argument, fought what must be the first-ever 'politics-lite' political campaign. Celebrities were wheeled out to show how really, really angry they were with Burberry for being such a nasty, nasty company. Conclusion? Celebrity gets street cred, politician gets pic in local paper, government gets off the hook, Burberry couldn't give a toss. Hey, everyone's happy – except the poor Burberry worker.

In the old days Labour politicians legislated to keep work in the UK, now they just line up for signed autographs from celebs. More celebrity politics than cerebral politics, it seems. The Burberry campaign used British nationalism to shame Burberry into giving the staff more redundancy pay. It also used class nationalism, tied in with the memory of the 1984 Miner's Strike, to paint the workers as the victims. Hmm. And I thought patriotism/nationalism was supposed to be the last refuge of the scoundrel. And I thought too, from what my British left-wing friends told me, that the whole point of Wales staying part of the UK was that this big state was stronger than capital. But it's not, so what's the point of Britain?

Of course, anyone dull enough to fight an Assembly election on an avidly socialist agenda will not win by pointing out the pit-falls of globalisation on communities like the Rhondda. Why? Because the electorate, like the politicians, are hypocrites too. I've been there. In a previous life I was a failed politician. I've tried convincing the public that we can legislate to keep jobs, and you know what? A blank, slightly patronising face looks back at your own earnest one. The public just don't buy it. In their bones they don't buy it. It's all bunkum. The British Left has no new philosophy, only policies. The Welsh nationalist left wing has the old philosophy, it's just that nobody believes in it any more.

The Left has lost the intellectual battle to the Right. And like in the Rhondda, it's the Left with class-jingoism and red flag waving. As a sign of its desperation for some political legitimacy, the Left campaigns on its own version of fighting foreign wars: saving little children in Africa, supporting various third-world revolutionaries, fighting past wars about Slavery and the Holocaust, and regurgitating the politics of the 1980s. The other battles have been lost intellectually or at the ballot box.

As the Assembly gains more power, as English and Scottish nationalisms rise, and as the implications of demographic and environmental change kick in, Welsh politicians will be forced, against their will, to move away from the policies of bribery and gimmicks and towards more substantial, strategic policies. Flying the 'bloodied flag' of class nationalism won't be enough. Welsh politics will also become more right wing and realistic and less about past tribalism. It's a pity there isn't a Welsh Gaullist party to champion this change.

Change will come, but for it to happen the generation of the 1980s will have to bequeath its duffle coats and protest stickers to a glass case at the Museum of Welsh Life at Saint Fagans and bin the bunk they've dined out on for the last twenty years. Who knows, with such newfound honesty and realism, maybe more people will bother voting, too?

There are many lessons to learn from the 1980s – some good and some bad, but it isn't just Margaret Thatcher and American-football-style shoulder padding that should do the apologising. Until everyone comes clean about the 1980s I will save any nostalgia for worthier causes, and I'd prefer the media not to go on reminding me of that awful decade – unless they want to be sued.

Cambria, volume 9, number 1, April-May 2007

This was a tricky one. An article about the grammar of Welsh, written in English for an audience who didn't speak Welsh! It was a little like asking the reader to watch a game of snooker on black and white television.

However, I took a punt that many readers would have some understanding of the language ... if only having been frustrated in long-ago lessons at school, or a tourist, or perennial adult learner.

There's also a lot of talk of the politics of language in Wales, and political status for Welsh is gaining incrementally. But there is less talk about the changing nature of the language many of us are trying to save! So, this is an article which tries to get under the skin of Welsh, and I hope raises some interesting questions for speakers of other languages, including English.

The debate is: how much should standard Welsh accept change and recognise it, and how much should it stand against change? Where's the Welsh language's line in the sand? And how does it deal with the incoming tide of English language dominance?

In December 2010 Alun Ffred Jones AM, Minister for Heritage, saw the new Welsh Language Act discussed in this article passed by the Assembly.

Vulgar Welsh

The Portuguese have just done it, the Germans are not happy with it and the Cornish have done in just two years what most languages take up to five hundred to do. Quite a few of the world's languages are updating or rewriting their grammatical rules and spelling. Is it time Welsh did so too?

I'm no linguist, but since it's over ninety years since the publication of the great John Morris Jones's *Orgraff yr Iaith Gymraeg* ('The Orthography of the Welsh Language') I think it's time to re-open the discussion.

But why consider making changes now and what would those changes be?

Politically and legally, the language is again under discussion, and there will be a new Welsh Act of some sort to follow those of 1967 and 1993. And so, the need for a consistent, easy-to-understand standard language has never been stronger . . . or more important.

Of course, standard Welsh already exists and has a noble tradition, one which shows its ability to adapt and make the right choices. Standard Welsh is ultimately based on the Welsh used in strict metre poetry (*cynghanedd*) and the Welsh laws. This is the Welsh that William Morgan developed for his Bible in 1588. In terms of orthography, if Morgan had had his way Cymraeg would be spelt Kymraeg. But as the Bible was printed in London, using English-language typefaces, he was forced to use 'c' because, as he said, 'the printers have not so many as the Welsh requireth' of the letter k. Morgan also wished to use 'x' for our 'ch' – 'x' is the Greek letter for the sound. A farsighted decision of Morgan's was to write Welsh words as they are pronounced rather than according to their etymology.

The lack of status for Welsh in authority and education led to competing and arbitrary orthographies by the nineteenth century. This was such a problem that a committee was set-up at the National Eisteddfod at Bangor in 1890 to tidy things up. Among their most sensible decisions was the excellent idea to get rid of all doubling of the letters 'm' and 't'. It was from this committee that John Morris Jones ultimately published his hugely influential and masterly *Orgraff yr Iaith Gymraeg* in 1928, which set the rules for modern standard written Welsh. However, the strain on standard Welsh became acute in the 1960s. The need to teach an accessible, standard version of the language to new learners led to the publication of the controversial guidebook, *Cymraeg Byw*, in 1964 that gave status to a more colloquial Welsh and recognised different accents in teaching programmes. I'd argue there will need to be another serious reassessment of the language's orthography of the size of John Morris Jones's contribution within the next twenty years.

Why? Well, our old friend demography again.

Demographic change affects Welsh in a pincer movement which make it impossible for Welsh not to consider its standard form over the next decade or so. The first is the decline of Welsh-speaking communities, towns and villages which were until a generation ago essentially monolingual Welsh in everyday speech. The second, on a more positive but equally far-reaching note, is the happy increase in Welsh-speakers from non-Welsh-speaking backgrounds, be they as pupils in the education system or adults learning the language.

As a result of this pincer movement significant forces over the last two generations have accelerated change in the very body of Welsh grammar. These changes, at least as regards the Welsh spoken by some sections of society, are maybe approaching the scale of the great transformation between the sixth and ninth centuries when Welsh emerged from Brythonic.

It seems to me that the experience of Welsh today within parts of Welsh society is similar to what happened to Dutch in southern Africa as it became Afrikaans. People whose second language was Dutch (Malays, Khoi or San), and whose grasp of Dutch was weak, raised Dutch children on the Cape. These second-language Dutch-speakers adapted the language, simplified it, added to it and created a new language, Afrikaans, and passed it back to the native Dutch speakers and especially the children. The dynamics here in Wales are different, of course. Welsh isn't the high status language, as Dutch was to the Malays. But the interplay between a growing section of the Welsh-speaking community which is native Welsh-speaking and those who are not is having a profound effect on the language, especially among children and especially in the south and north-east.

The demography gives a clue to the reason for what's happening. Although figures can be hard to come by, more than twice the number of children under ten who speak Welsh come from non-Welsh-speaking backgrounds as from Welsh-speaking ones. And of the wildly optimistic 40 per cent whose parents claimed their five- to fifteen-year-olds could speak Welsh in the 2001 census, other figures show that only 20 per cent of children pass Key Stage 1 in Welsh and 14 per cent for Key Stage 3, which gives some indication of the fluency of those speakers. Such a big demographic change, coupled with a sometime weak grasp of aspects of the language, is sure to have an effect on the development of Welsh.

It's commonplace to point out that of the global population who speak English today, only 20 per cent speak it as a first language. Linguists like Professor David Crystal point out that this will have an effect not only on the type of English spoken in the future, but even on the very cadence of the language. If this demographic fact is true of English is it not naive, or self-denial, to say that Welsh, which may soon be spoken by a large minority or even majority of people who speak it as a second language, will also be affected?

If this is so, and if we really want to see Welsh more widely used in all spheres of life we cannot just rely on muscular and innovative language teaching and new laws to increase the status of the language. Vital though these are, we must be open to the possible need to reform the standard of the language itself in the future.

I will leave those better qualified than myself to discuss

the details, but I'll make some observations.

The great beauty of the Welsh language for me is its spelling – the great gift of our forefathers. So fantastically elastic, so wonderful in its common sense and athleticism. A few more simplifications would make it perfect. The most obvious is to ditch the surviving double 'n' and 'r'. After all, the Bangor committee dropped the double 't' and 'm' and it's been no great loss, so why micro-manage the pronunciation of the language by retaining the double 'r' and 'n'?

There are some minor rules set down by John Morris Jones which seem today almost arbitrary. Other quirks of the language, however, lead to incitement to grammatical hatred, creating a culture among learners of expecting grammatical trap-doors when, in fact, there aren't that many.

Which brings me on to mutations – the regular consonant changes that occur at the beginning of Welsh words. Many languages have mutations of some sort, including Hebrew and even English. The tendency of many English speakers to pronounce 'little' as 'liddle' follows the Welsh language's soft mutation rules (t > d) for instance. So English mutates in the middle of words, and for similar reasons, one presumes, Welsh-speakers found it easier (lazier, maybe?) to mutate at the beginning of words. It is believed our modern mutations developed during the change from Brythonic to Welsh from the sixth century onwards. During this period Brythonic underwent massive transformation; nouns went from three genders (like in today's German) to two. Word endings and cases (used in Latin and many Indo-European languages of the time), were shortened or lost, shifting the accent of words and leading ultimately to the smorgasbord of ways to pluralise in Welsh and to the mutations we know and love.

Mutations are the shibboleth of the Welsh language, infuriating and fascinating Welsh-speakers in equal measure.

We can't be without them, they're in our DNA – a fact underlined by the birth of a new mutation during the last decades. Two 'alien' sounds to Welsh, the English 'tch' and 'j' tango to create the as yet unnamed mutation of 'tch' > j as exemplified in the unromantic and decidedly urban, '*bag o jips*' (yes, it does mean 'a bag of chips'!).

However, people are gradually voting with their tongues and will try in increasing numbers, in true rugby-fashion, to side-step mutations. That great rugby outside half bastion, the Gwendraeth Valley in Carmarthenshire, have declared UDI against the nasal mutation. People in Pontyberem won't normally use the correct nasal mutation '*yng Nghaerfyrddin*' (in Carmarthen) but rather the incorrect soft mutation '*yn Gaerfyrddin*'. The same is true in Caernarfon. These are local colloquialisms and mostly tolerated (orally at least), maybe because they are by now an accepted part of the local accent. Whatever the reason as the academic Mari Jones (among many) has noted in her 1998 study of spoken Welsh, this mutation, the nasal mutation, is heard less and less. It's either passed over for the soft mutation as above, or sentences are constructed to as to avoid mutating at all.

The mutation-averse grammar is exemplified by putting the possessive pronoun '*fy*' (my) after the noun. So, '*fy nhad*' (my father) can be avoided by saying '*tad fi*'; '*fy nghar*' (my car) '*car fi*'. Clever see? This is growing in use despite it often being easier to actually mutate – saying '*nhad*' (implying '*fy nhad*') is surely quicker than 'my dad' or even '*dad fi*'. This has the effect of fingernails down a blackboard for most Welsh teachers but isn't wholly without sense. After all, we say '*car Siôn*' (Siôn's car) so why not '*car fi*'?

It's difficult to see the nasal mutation lasting much more than a generation in everyday speech, especially in the southeast. When will our standard grammar recognise this – and *should* it? And that's the big question. We all have our linguistic hobbyhorses or pet dislikes. When, why and who should accommodate these changes?

Mutation is one point, vocabulary another. Sensitive to catcalls that Welsh has no word for 'entrepreneurs' (as one person actually told me), we like to create new words; though funnily enough, Welsh 'invents' new words whilst English new words arrive by divine birth. We believe that there is no new concept in the world that our ancestors hadn't premeditated and given us words for, or compound words, to describe them. These neologisms, especially in the field of the internet, are often clever and expressive, for instance, '*cluniadur*' (laptop or 'lapter' if you like) is one of my favourites. But I do sometimes feel we could just borrow the Latin or Greek word like almost everyone else does. Why not '*ecspres*' or '*ecstra*' if the context fits, rather than '*cyflym*' or '*ychwanegol*' in advertising or slogans where the product is branded, not just described?

One could define a non-standard language as one which has no word for a battleship. Welsh isn't at that stage, nor close to it. Despite centuries of official neglect and even discrimination, it has an adaptive and democratic standard language which can accommodate nuances in social and regional differences. But beneath the surface there is also a strong current of change. Through education and status, this *koine* can be channelled towards using a standard and robust Welsh but we need also be aware that it is a swelling current. Our language leaders could maybe begin by taking a look at the most common mistakes and ask are there understandable reasons for these beyond weak teaching skills?

Is it possible for the language to adapt where needed but concentrate its energy and genius in developing new words, new similes, new forms of expression? Or do we lose both if we lose one? On the centenary of John Morris Jones's

Orgraff in 2028 we will need a new standard Welsh; a Welsh that doesn't seem foreign to the thousands of new Welsh-speakers, but which is also a Welsh that is happy in its own skin.

Cambria, volume 10, number 5, January–February 2009

OK, it's time to come out of the closet: if not a fan, I've always been admirer of the royal family's ability to put on a good show, from a wedding to a funeral. On a Welsh scale, then only the Gorsedd of the Bards comes close, but even that's a long way removed from the royals.

The truth is, everyone likes a bit of pomp and ceremony, and it's only the political connotations that go with it that stops a minority of Welsh people from enjoying it.

The British state understands the reasoning behind pomp and ceremony. It's cultural shock and awe; make your opponents cower, and straighten the backs of your supporters. That's why they do it. That's why all states do it. You can't change human nature. It's performance theatre at its best; street entertainment at its most impressive, interactive history at its most accessible, entertainment at its cheapest.

It's time we Welsh learned to celebrate and hang out our brightest colours if we wish to buy people into the national project.

Hang out our brightest colours

A lack of things to actually celebrate is, admittedly, a prime cause of our nation's sad state of affairs. We haven't won too many battles, haven't won a world cup, and we don't even compete in the smiles-and-sequins chauvinism which is the Eurovision Song Contest. We seem to be in perpetual depression about the state of our language or economy.

And when we do celebrate, the probability is that one half of the nation doesn't agree with the celebration – it being either too Welsh, too English, too militaristic or too religious for one or other of our various tribes. And, what's worse, not only are we not very good at celebrating, but we're not too good at being morose and miserable either! Miserable

American blacks created the blues, miserable poor white Portuguese the fado, and the Welsh . . . *cerdd dant*! Heavens! Our inability to celebrate our nationality contrasts startlingly with the Irish. Am I the only one who admits to periods of feeling a little short-changed when I compare our limp St David's Day celebrations with the full-blown Irish commitment to St Patrick's Day? Everyone, it seems, celebrates St Patrick's Day: even Welsh people go out for a drink on St Pat's, but not on St Dai's.

But then, isn't that St Patrick Day's weakness as well? If celebrating St Pat's is more acceptable to some Welsh people than celebrating St Dai's, is that such a sad indictment on our country? Or is it a thing of power, in that Welshness is still an identity in a state of contention, an identity which asks questions of us? With due respect to my Irish republican friends, isn't celebrating St Patrick's Day today more 'British' than celebrating St David's Day? And therefore, isn't it more generally acceptable to celebrate 'Irishness' than to celebrate 'Welshness'? Isn't it a fact that Welsh identity is less culturally 'acceptable' and more risqué than Irish identity?

And what's so special about getting drunk on your patron saint's day, in any case? In today's twenty-four hour drink culture, how is that so different from any other weekend? The more I think about it, the more I enjoy the succulently ascetic quality of St David's Day. We celebrate our patron saint with poetry and lectures in drafty village halls. Children take part in school eisteddfodau where literature, art and music are elevated. Despite the patriot's wariness of the bombast of the St David's Day Welshmen, there is still strength in the smell of wilting leeks and crusty Welsh Cakes.

And yet, there is also a feeling of under-achievement and of frustrated passion. I don't wish for the tardiness which is St Patrick's, but I do yearn for some colour and pageant and, do you know what, I don't think I'm the only one.

For most of the twentieth century, Welsh Labourism saw Wales not as a nation with a culture and language but as a population just waiting to be ill or unemployed. Our identity was as walking potential patients. But my identity isn't defined by ailment or occupation, and despite the modernist prophesies, neither is any one else's. I don't march in solidarity and celebration with other rheumatoid arthritis sufferers. Gone are yesteryear's Miners' Galas, and do their grandchildren march behind the banner of the Allied Beauty Therapists and Suntan Operators or Assistant Human Resource Managers today? No, but the call of Dewi is still there – and getting louder. Identity politics will be the political ballast of the next generation. The politics of being Welsh – the concern for language and culture – will be the politics of the world.

The media has always used St David's Day as a peg for a 'Welsh Story' – my tip, don't bother launching anything on March 1st because the Welsh establishment will always gazump your story. 2008 saw the official opening of our monolingual 'Senedd', a name objected to by two monoglot English-cultural-nationalist Assembly Members.

Celebrating the opening of the Senedd was an act of political ventriloquism. We were celebrating a National Assembly building whose aesthetic is post-national, a building whose 'transparent' architecture was dated before it was opened; a cathedral without Christ.

Thankfully, the third annual St David's Day Parade, which was held through the streets of the capital, saved the day. It was a fantastic celebration in the spirit of Iolo Morganwg. Some may sneer at the parade's 'Welsh Horse', the cavalry resplendent in the red and green tunics of the Welsh Cavalry of the Great War. Some may laugh at the walkers wearing the 'Welsh cilt' (and yes, a blatant case of cultural plagiarism if ever there was one). Others may squirm at the Welsh bagpipes or tut-tut at the proud hoisting of St David's flag. But why? Life can be pretty dull; we'll all die some time, so why not celebrate while we can? Why not dress up for special occasions? Must we for ever wear our heritage like a hair shirt? Why let our hang-ups about celebrating our nationality with pageantry haunt us?

Parades need not be expressions only of nationality, of course. Diverse communities from gays to Catholics in Wales have recognised the importance of the public display of a procession. And if their communal parades can be celebrated, then why not the national community? Why the slight embarrassment or twitching condescension by some of our intellectuals?

The 'Welsh cilt' is as Welsh, or as unWelsh, as rugby or triple harps once were. The mistake its promoters make is to claim that it's 'traditional' or 'Welsh' – it's not, but then we don't need an excuse to dress up! If our people ape the latest Paris fashion or the look of black America with their back-to-front baseball caps and baggy trousers, why not follow the fashion of other nations too? Wearing a 'Welsh cilt' is no more ridiculous or false than wearing a 'Welsh' rugby jersey or 'Welsh' tall hat, and is certainly better than the ghastly class-ridden parody of the top hat and tails.

Welshmen playing the invented 'Welsh' bagpipes are no more false or contrite than white Welsh intellectuals playing the jazz tunes of black Americans. If a Welshman can be inspired by American blues then can he not also be inspired by Scottish or Breton music as well? For some reason, a section of the Welsh left wing sees this whole cultural movement as sinister and distasteful if not verging on the fascistic. Is that the reason that no Assembly Member of the Labour Party has turned up at any of the previous St David's Day Parades, despite members from all three other parties enjoying the day?

This most recent exciting development in our culture is a breath of fresh air. Rather than just culturally passively swallowing American culture whole – the blues, jazz or bluegrass of the left-wing intellectuals or the rap and pop of the young and working class – a growing number of Welsh people are actively processing cultures from beyond our border and beyond Anglo-Americaland. The anti-culture AMs who complain that their constituents have no cultural facilities are the ones who've stood on the outside, sneering at the beautiful movement of Welsh cultural renaissance. A renaissance movement which asked, 'Why are we singing other people's songs, in another people's languages or accents about places we've never been to?'

The new-found urge to celebrate our patron saint's day openly is answering the deep call of a nation increasingly looking beyond the narrow six-generation historiography of the British left wing, and discovering two millennia of myth and history. It's a movement which is unstoppable and which will have far-reaching repercussions.

In Wales, where every second town and village has been named after a saint, if we were to be honest with ourselves and put a stop to our continuous self-loathing and self-deprecation, would we not come to the door of the Eastern Orthodox church, a religion that venerates the saints? The Eastern Orthodox church, like no other, is truly in tune with the yearning for a sense of place, history and spirituality. In the long view of our millennia history, wasn't Nonconformity but a two-century nap? Are we Welsh not Celts but Slavs?

But even whilst honouring the celebration of Dewi I still feel it's not quite the appropriate way to remember our patron saint. 1922 was the year our Irish cousins formed their Free State. Likewise, 1922 was an important date for us, as it was the year we disestablished the Anglican Church;

Wales, in its own, quiet self-deprecating way, separated church and state. Should we not now also do the same with St David's Day?

I can't help feeling that old Dewi has for too long had the whole weight of a nation on his shoulders. Now that we have our Senedd, isn't it time we unburdened him a little and let him walk tall as a Christian and not as a Welshman? Must every new Welsh 'initiative' be launched on St David's Day? Must we mix religion with nationality? After all, the two aren't the same, either from a Welsh atheist, Welsh Muslim or Welsh Jew's point of view.

Should we not celebrate St David's Day as a truly Christian saint's day, a day maybe of pilgrimage to his holy sites or to remember his work and legacy? And if so, should we not have another purely secular day to celebrate our ancient nation? That day should be not only a celebration of the tenacity of our language and nationality, but also a celebration of its evolving dynamism. It should be a day not marking a defeat in battle or partisan politics but a day which celebrates a unified nation. Better still, should it not be held during a warmer season of our gloriously disrespectful Welsh climate? Shouldn't that day be the day a Welshman was proclaimed Prince of Wales in 1400 – 16 September, Owain Glyndŵr Day?

But why stop there? In the spirit of the Welsh Orthodox church, why not local celebrations of local saints; Teilo, Illtud, Padarn, Cybi? Their dates are in T. D. Breverton's fascinating publication, *The Book of Welsh Saints* (WalesBooks, 2000). We have no need to rely on bog-snorkelling gimmicks for other festive days either. We already have the Mari Lwyd and Calennig customs for New Year, St Dwynwen on the 25th January is our Valentine's Day, Cilmeri on 11 December for our heroic dead, and what happened to Dic Penderyn, Hywel Dda, the Chartists or

Merched Beca? And should not old Iolo also be celebrated – the man who gave us so much colour?

The Jews are a people to be admired. Isn't the genius of their longevity as a people down to two master-strokes: first, the matrilineal law whereby Jewishness is passed through the female line, and second, their myriad festivals and commemorations? These festivals draw the community together in strength and hope. They are festivals which also draw the family together and celebrate the importance of family, the conductor of morals, tradition and language – an entity far more powerful and important than any state, community – and, yes, nation. Isn't it time we also had a day to celebrate the Welsh family?

Dewi placed a handkerchief beneath his feet at Llanddewi Brefi so that the earth rose and all could see and hear what he had to say. If we're serious about ourselves isn't it time we also used cloth, in our brightest colours, not to place beneath our feet, but to fly and wear for all to see our pride in our nation? Dewi also famously said, 'Gwnewch y pethau bychain', 'Do the small things'. He didn't say '*Meddyliwch yn fychan*', 'Think small'. It's time we thought big and started celebrating – big time!

Cambria, volume 8, number 1, March–April 2006

The whole argument which flared up after Cllr Seimon Glyn's remarks on BBC Radio Wales in February 2001 (see below) changed the course of Welsh politics and the whole nature of debate. For some two years after that, any remark, however innocent, was fed into the narrative of the 'nationalist as racist'. There was the almost comical situation where speakers of English could claim to be maltreated by Welsh racists in much the same way as poor Pakistani workers would, whilst simultaneously claiming that there was no need to learn Welsh, as their language, English, had the prestige and status of the state.

The author Andrew Hammond in his book The Debated Lands – British and American Representations of the Balkans (University of Wales Press, 2007) brought to my attention a word new to me, 'balkanism'. It is used to define a set of prejudices which is conveniently and lazily used to signify some ready-known clichés which are unique and consistent to the area, from the so-called 'ethnic hatred' to 'deception' and 'laziness'. In much the same way any discussion about the future of the Welsh language as a living community language was fed into a ready-made narrative as 'nationalist as racist'.

As so many social and political commentators don't speak Welsh (even those writing about Wales) and some harbour the same set of 'balkanisms' about Welsh society, I felt it was important to put in print an alternative and truer picture. As Simon Brooks noted, deliberate mistranslations in the tabloid press were taken as gospel, then used as citations by distinguished academics, and then taken as fact by the outside world. The 'nationalist as racist' narrative, like that of 'balkanism', feeds ignorance and prejudice and is an obstruction to healthy debate and understanding. It belittles people and their cultures ... which of course was the whole point.

Beyond the Pale: the deliberate misuse and abuse of the term 'racism'

The Idiom of Dissent (published by Gomer Press, 2006) isn't a book most people would pack away with their towels and sunglasses as they prepare for their summer holiday, but if you're interested in the manipulation of the media in Wales, one chapter makes interesting reading.

In a chapter called 'The Idioms of Race: the "racist nationalist" in Wales as bogeyman', Simon Brooks, former editor of Welsh-language current affairs journal *Barn*, outlined the 'Newspeak' used by the Labour party to create the 'racist nationalist' phantom to save its own electoral skin. It's a chapter which shone a spotlight on one of the shabbiest periods in Welsh political life.

At its heart it exposed the colonial attitude towards the Welsh language by many journalists and politicians, the weakness of the Welsh media community, and the sheer laziness of individual journalists and even academics.

The chapter recalled the events following the 'Seimon Glyn Affair'. Readers may recall that Seimon Glyn, a Plaid Cymru councillor on Gwynedd Council, commented on a BBC Radio Wales phone-in (on 17th January 2001) that the movement of English people to Welsh-speaking villages was changing the language of the villages. He suggested that there wouldn't be a problem if there was a monitoring of that movement, and that people moving into those areas were made aware of Welsh culure and were persuaded (or made) to learn Welsh.

Glyn was instantly branded 'anti-English' and 'racist', even though north Wales' Chief Constable Richard Brunstrom concluded in September 2001 that 'there is no evidence you intended to created racial hatred' and that at the heart of Glyn's comments was a concern for language, not race. Astonishingly, Seimon Glyn was all but lynched for stating the bleeding obvious, and for making what were, with hindsight, some totally unremarkable comments. His assertion and concern was that the movement of significant numbers of people from a strong linguistic community (English) into an area of a language with low prestige was going to weaken that smaller language community (Welsh).

Labour politicians habitually asked people to substitute 'Pakistani' for 'English' and see the racial correlation. As they well knew, it would have been more instructive to substitute the word 'Welsh' with 'Tibetan' or another smaller stateless language, and 'English' with 'Chinese' or some other larger and more prestigious state language. It is to the eternal shame of the Commission of Racial Equality, a body of high prestige and power within the Labour Party, that such simple and obvious points weren't made at the outset of the Affair, something which might have led to a more enlightening debate.

But no difference; Seimon Glyn was just the wrong man in the wrong place concerned about the wrong language. Following Plaid Cymru's surprise success in the first National Assembly elections of May 1999, it seems that as early as September of that year, the Labour Party in Wales decided on a strategy of creating the 'racist nationalist bogeyman', with the Welsh language becoming the Welsh equivalent of the Orange Card (the Ulster Unionists' refusal to join Northern Ireland into a United Ireland).

The Labour Party strategy was ruthlessly implemented and set the tone of debate in the press. Genuine racial attacks which occurred at the time were given scant coverage in comparison with the perceived 'racial' debate which swirled around the Welsh language. The continuation of the 'racist-nationalist bogeyman' narrative gave the prejudice an air of authenticity. As the political lecturer Dr Richard Wyn Jones noted, a 'Big Lie' can be accepted as 'Truth' when it is repeated and not challenged. In Wales The Big Lie went virtually unchallenged, in part due to Plaid Cymru's weak leadership having a virtual political nervous breakdown in the wake of Seimon Glyn's comments. The defence of Seimon Glyn and the whole concept of the survival of Welsh-speaking areas was left to individuals with little political clout, no financial backing and little power or control of the mass media. This was a fact of which the notorious Labour-supporting *Welsh Mirror* was fully aware. And it was able ruthlessly to exploit this in the knowledge that neither Seimon Glyn nor his supporters would have the strength or the financial resources to seek redress against any libellous comments, nor have the means of reaching the mass of the Welsh population, without having to express themselves through the distorted prism of the 'established' racist-nationalist narrative.

Labour's attack covered several sections of the media at several levels, all indicating a ruthlessness and vindictiveness honed after years in opposition in Britain and, ironically, after years of similar libel and targeted lies by the London Tory press in the 1980s. It could, of course, be argued that politics is a rough game and 'all's fair in war'. However, putting aside the moral and political worth of the idiotic invective which the likes of Labour's Ken Livingstone – and even Neil Kinnock – had to put up with in the 1980s, and the dubious morality of applying the same tactics when in power, the 'discourse' was hardly on a level playing field. The very weakness of the Welsh language and the general ignorance of its dire situation within Wales – not to mention outside – gave the Labour Party all the best cards. Welsh was given a weak hand with weak players.

The very day after Seimon Glyn made his comments, the *Welsh Mirror*, the Labour Party's organ of choice, screamed

'Voice of Hate' in banner headlines, giving absolutely no representation at all to the passionate concern felt by tens of thousands for the future of the Welsh language. This set the ball rolling and Labour invested in it heavily. On 28 January 2001, under the title: 'Exposed: A Web of Deceit', *Wales on Sunday* reported how Labour's London Millbank headquarters was found to have sent 1,275 messages, under pseudonyms, to a Welsh politics chat room to turn up the heat of the political debate, and had fabricated quotes attributed to Plaid Cymru members.

In March, a Plaid Councillor from the Rhondda was slated for condemning British imperialism, because in doing so he had accused the 'English' of having 'raped ... every country that they've been in'. Two months later Leanne Wood, a Plaid general election candidate, was accused in the *Welsh Mirror*, with no sense of irony whatsoever, of 'whipping up hatred'. Under the *Mirror's* title of 'Plaid War of Hate', Wood's crime was calling Labour a 'British nationalist party' – which, of course, strictly-speaking it is, and which is confirmed by comments and policies on nationality and language by Blair, Brown and Blunkett, in addition to Welsh Labour AMs. Again, she was just stating the bleeding obvious.

The misrepresentation and faux horror on comments made by various nationalists was a case of playing hard-ball with politics – a fact which Leanne Wood understood only too well and tried to counter, whilst the leaders of Plaid tried in vain and fear to be more 'reasonable', and by doing so gave credibility to Labour's slurs. Labour's tactics certainly put Plaid on the back foot. The calls of racism verged on the ridiculous and became a parody of itself. As the commentator Patrick McGuiness noted in *Planet* (Issue 159, June/July 2003), the term 'racism' was used 'in politics and media for everything from supporting the Welsh football team to the Welsh language act, from advertising jobs that require fluency in Welsh to S4C's lack of subtitles'.

The Labour party also employed a Welsh-speaker to trawl and mis-translate articles written in Welsh. This person (or persons) who, in the spirit of Nazi and racist parlance of the time, can perhaps be justifiably described as 'quislings' à propos their language, gladly sold Welsh for a few pieces of silver and votes.

Beca Brown, the daughter of English parents who moved to Gwynedd and learned Welsh, was one of many to feel the heat due to Labour's selective translation. In an article in *Barn* (July/August 2001) entitled '*O ba beth a gwnaethpwyd hiliaeth*' ('of what is racism made') Brown dealt openly and honestly with the whole question of 'race' and identity. As a member of a minority, she wrote, she harboured 'racist' feelings towards a 'colonial' majority. Such feelings were unacceptable and had to be challenged: 'racism breeds bullying – and we have to release ourselves from this terrible cycle'. *Wales on Sunday* printed a doctored translation of her text – translating '*cenedl*' (nation) as 'race' but chose to edit out the final paragraph which condemned such 'racism' as bullying. As Brooks notes, it would be interesting to know if the translation was *Wales on Sunday*'s own or if it was a doctored copy supplied by Labour.

Mis-translating '*cenedl*' for race was one popular trick which both the *Welsh Mirror* and Labour knew the vast majority of people would never quite pick up on, and by the time anyone got round to complaining it would be too late. The damage would have been done. Brooks himself was mistranslated. In an editorial in March 2002 he talked of 'civil disobedience' (*anufudd-dod sifil*) only to see the Labour party release a 'translation' via a press release with the term changed to 'civil disorder' with images of war-torn states! It was somewhat ironic in such circumstances to hear Labour politicians like Don Touhig lecturing Plaid about reading more Martin Luther King!

Even when Welsh nationalists showed hostility to those with genuine anti-Welsh racist tendencies who had moved into Wales, it was the Welsh nationalists who were painted as the villains by Labour. One famous case of dirty tricks happened at the Meifod National Eisteddfod and was reported extensively on the BBC on 8 August 2003 (perhaps the BBC was smarting from Labour's claim in the *Welsh Mirror* on 20 June 2002: 'Biased Broadcasting Channel: Station accused of being "pro-nationalist"'). The 'English race claim', as the BBC termed it, was based on the selective interpretation of a quote by Plaid Cymru President, Dafydd Iwan, and given to the station by the Labour party. Dafydd Iwan's concern that elements of the racist 'white flight' from multicultural urban conurbations in England was one factor why people were moving to rural Wales, was turned on its head, suggesting that Dafydd Iwan supported the 'white flight' and almost welcomed such people and prejudices!

Very soon the whole canvas of Welsh language culture was being labelled inherently racist, being described, once again with no hint of irony, by one Labour AM as 'beyond the Pale' (the 'Pale' being the ring around English-controlled Dublin that excluded the Irish). Professor Dafydd Glyn Jones, a distinguished and diligent academic, was almost censored from giving evidence at an Assembly Committee to discuss the Language in May 2001. Huw Lewis, Labour AM for Merthyr, said Assembly committees might have to consider 'outrageous, sexist, xenophobic, racist, inflammatory, even illegal statements in the future'. The Labour Education Minister, Jane Davidson, suggested that evidence might have to be vetted beforehand. The idea was rejected following legal advice, but it shows the Labour mindset – the aim was not just to rebut language arguments, but by using the 'race-language' discourse, to delegitimise them, thus debasing any sensible discussion about the future of the Welsh language and Welsh cultural life in general. It was that which was really 'beyond the Pale'.

Welsh language activists were labelled 'language loonies' or 'language nutters'. The Welsh language became a 'secret code' and Welsh-language articles were published 'under the cover of the Welsh language' ('Bigots Harm Wales', *Welsh Mirror*, June 22, 2001). Even the National Eisteddfod became, infamously, the 'Festival of Fear and Hatred' (*Welsh Mirror*, August 2, 2002) – which must have been startling news to the girls performing the floral dance, or the thousands of visitors, including many thousands of non-Welsh speakers and Welsh people from around the world.

Compare these patently nonsensical comments with the complete absence of similar expressions of opprobrium towards those communities in England which recently elected members of the unashamedly racist BNP. Soon, we will no doubt see the 'issues' and 'concerns' raised by these BNP-voting constituencies climb their way up the Labour policy ladder, as have other so-called 'issues' which Labour once labelled xenophobic or nationalistic. Welsh nationalism seems almost alone in being the only 'right wing' set of policies not adopted by Labour since 1997.

Labour's great success however, was that the Big Lie became accepted in general parlance within academic and 'respectable' circles. The 'racist nationalist' sobriquet made its way through the corridors of academia and the social sciences. Part of the problem, of course, as Brooks acknowledges in his article, is that 'while secondary source material exists in English, most of the primary source material is in Welsh' – a language many of those who spout the nonsense about 'racist nationalism' haven't been bothered to learn. Might this be because of their own deep-seated colonial attitudes towards Welsh?

A key figure in the academic canonisation of the 'racist nationalist' myth has been the respected and much-liked academic Charlotte Williams. However, in Planet (the editor of which might have asked her to consult the original article in its original language) Williams shoddily repeated the erroneous suggestion lifted straight out of *Wales on Sunday* that Beca Brown hates the English 'as a race'. Here was an example of the 'racist nationalist' idiom following through, like a convolvulus in the garden, all the way from doctored translation (by whom, one wonders?) via tabloid exposé to academic 'fact'. In her seminal book, *A Tolerant Nation?* – a leading academic study of multiculturalism and race relations in Wales – Williams still accuses Seimon Glyn of 'racist terminology'

Five years on and what's changed? Well, Labour 'won' that particular war. Good on them! Plaid Cymru lost five seats and Rhodri Morgan was back as First Minister. That Plaid Cymru failed to take an effective stand against Labour is neither here or there. Politics is a tough game and parties come and go. That's Plaid's problem. Though the whole affair derailed any serious debate – which was the whole point, of course. The tragedy of the whole episode is that despite the apparent efforts at creating a 'bilingual Wales', the last remaining Welsh-speaking (that is, bilingual) communities are disappearing under the dual weights of British capitalism and Brown's housing boom – a subject Labour made sure we couldn't discuss. On a happier note, the Commission for Racial Equality has made great strides away from their previous, and at times, colonial attitude towards the Welsh language, and began discussions with Cymuned (the movement founded in support of Seimon Glyn); and the CRE Director in Wales, Chris Myant, spoke at a Cymdeithas yr Iaith, 'Welsh – Equal rights?' lobby in the

National Assembly in 2006.

However, the most galling feature emerging from all this is the rank hypocrisy of the Labour party. Genuine issues and concerns raised by Seimon Glyn about the obvious and de facto movement of people were branded 'racist' or 'beyond the Pale' in a discussion about a language under threat, yet the very same concerns are quite openly debated when considering 'British' identity and values. Whilst Betty Williams, Labour MP for Conwy, taunted nationalists in 2002 saying 'You can't eat a flag', Scotsman Gordon Brown lectured us about the importance of flying the Union Jack in our gardens!

It was in 2001, the year of the Seimon Glyn Affair, that the Labour party began to voice the idea that there should be restrictions on non-English speakers gaining UK citizenship, and that immigrants would be required to learn English. By 2002, as Brooks notes, David Blunkett was calling for British Asians to 'speak English at home'. Indeed, proposals which established tougher regulatory frameworks for citizenship and language requirements became law as part of the 2002 Nationality, Immigration and Asylum Act.

The hypocrisy doesn't stop there. When a Labour leaflet was distributed in Cardiff during the 2004 local election campaign playing on prejudice against 'Travellers and Gypsies', Labour became the only political party in early twenty-first century Wales which was forced to apologise for using racist propaganda in an election campaign: ('Welsh Labour apologise for offensive leaflet', CRE website 29 September 2004). Readers will remember that while Seimon Glyn was cleared of making any 'racist remarks', Labour's xenophobia, openly revealed in the Cardiff leaflet, did not enter the discourse of political racism in Wales, whereas manufactured examples of bogus 'racist nationalism' were replayed in the media again and again.

Labour still peddles the lie of the 'racist-nationalist-bogeyman' and will, one fears, do so until the end of time, as it is an essential prerequisite of their own self-definition. One can only hope however, that students of media, politics and the social sciences, and, indeed the general public itself, will, in future be more circumspect, and refrain from swallowing the 'Big Lie which became the Truth'.

Cambria, volume 8, number 2, May–June 2006

Talk of punitive laws against the Welsh or obscure government reports into education should really be consigned to rather quirky questions in a game of Trivial Pursuit or a pub quiz. However, in Wales they're not, and that's because their effects are still felt. They're still relevant because unlike our friends in Eastern Europe, the Czechs, Estonians and Slovenes, who gained status for their own languages in the nineteenth century by setting up financial and commercial enterprises using them, the Welsh didn't. The failure to exorcise the ghosts of those laws meant that the effects of Welsh history are very much alive today, and nowhere more so than in the field of business.

Doing business in Welsh: 'Like asking for condoms!'

'There's no Welsh word for entrepreneur.'

Yes . . . and said without a hint of irony.

I couldn't believe it. Would I bother telling him that 'entrepreneur' was a French word?

What he was trying to say was that the Welsh language was incompatible with the business world. In that respect, the man's prejudice, or view, isn't unique. In fact, many Welsh-speakers may even agree with him.

With this in mind, I was very interested to read an article about the founding of the first designated Welsh-language bookshop. Not Siop y Pethe in Aberystwyth in the late 1960s, as I'd thought, but one opened a decade earlier in Llanrwst by Arianwen and Dafydd Parri. The article was written by their son, Myrddin ap Dafydd, who is himself the founder of a successful publishing and printing firm, Gwasg Carreg Gwalch, and has twice been chaired bard at the National Eisteddfod. The story of the establishment of that first bookshop in Llanrwst says a lot about the relationship between the Welsh language and business ... and shows how far things have moved on since the 1950s.

There was a constant concern after the Second World War about the decline in the sale of Welsh-language books. The opportunity to buy Welsh books was also decreasing as publishing houses stopped producing books in the language and shopkeepers who, had traditionally stocked Welsh books, gave priority to English newspapers and magazines.

However, Dafydd and Arianwen Parri saw this time, of all times, as a business opportunity. Newly returned from London, the young married couple settled down in Flintshire. Between 1953 and 1955 they saw a gap in the market and began selling Welsh books on a 'sale or return' basis from the back of an old post van in Llanrwst market and also at literary societies in Flintshire and the Chester area.

'I remember selling Gwasg y Brython Christmas cards in Holywell in 1954,' said Arianwen, who's now in her eighties. 'An old woman came to the stall and her eyes lit up as she saw them – she'd never seen Welsh-language greeting cards before and had never dreamt that such a thing was possible!'

Business was good. During his time selling books on Llanrwst's Square, Myrddin's father would take £50-worth of books to sell. On a good day he'd sell them all. That compared well with a teacher's monthly wage of £30. The pair bought the house and shop at Tan-y-graig in Llanrwst for £1,260 in 1955, and managed to clear the debt through the sales of selling Welsh merchandise and books in the first two or three years.

And it was on Llanrwst Square that the idea was born. Myrddin's father found a job at the nearby Pentrefoelas primary school and Myrddin's sister, Gwawr (the first of five children) was born in 1955 when the young family moved from Flintshire to Tan-y-graig. With Gwenno the three month old baby sleeping in old book boxes, Arianwen opened her 'Siop Llyfrau Cymraeg', putting empty boxes behind the books so that the shelves looked fuller!

Their success, no doubt came as a surprise to many of the pair's friends and family. Not that anyone denied the pair weren't industrious and good business people, but that they were doing so with such prominence to the Welsh language. To give a Welsh name to your business was a very unusual thing in the 1950s. As Myrddin says, to include the word 'Cymraeg' was even rarer. A few snippets sum up the peculiar, paradoxically repressed atmosphere of the 'you've never had it so good' era in Welsh-speaking Wales.

'One Monday, some weeks after opening the shop and in anticipation of the November fair week, my mother was clearing the old merchandise and placing new titles in the shop window. She overheard an old women tell her friend smugly as they passed, *'Mae hon yn cau, yli. Ro'n i'n deud wrthat ti mai dyna fasa'i hanas hi, yn do'n? Gormod o Gymraeg, yli.'* (This one's closing, see. I told you that's what would happen, didn't I? Too much Welsh, see).'

But close members of the family were also concerned about the *'gormod o Gymraeg'*. Myrddin's uncle, Ifan Owen of nearby Eglwys-bach, went into the shop one day, and suggested – in an incredibly nice way, of course – that there was too much Welsh on the sign outside and that was bad for business. Myrddin's parents had also just installed a telephone and had also written 'Ffôn' not 'Telephone' on the sign. Old Ifan agreed that it was very nice to come into a shop and be served in Welsh but added, *'Peidiwch â defnyddio gormod arni hi rhag i chi ddychryn pobol!'* ('Don't use it [Welsh] too much in case you scare people!').

To put this in context, the 1951 census showed that 81 per cent of the people of Llanrwst spoke Welsh – 6 per cent could speak only Welsh! For a rural market town in the 1950s and 60s the vast amount of their trade (even during tourist season) would have been local people, and the vast majority of them spoke Welsh. So who were they so afraid of offending? 'The attitude was still alive even twenty years later,' recalls Myrddin. 'By this time, Iorwerth, my mother's brother and his wife, Irene, ran a business selling Welsh-language greeting cards which they'd supply to shops across Wales. In several areas the shopkeepers would refuse to exhibit Welsh language cards, *'rhag pechu yn erbyn y Saeson, chi'n gw'bod'* ('so as not to offend English people, y'know'). The cards would be kept in boxes under the counter and the customer would have ask for them, *'fel gofyn am gondoms'* ('like asking for condoms') as Iorwerth would say!'

Who were these mysterious people who'd be frightened by the Welsh language? As Myrddin recalls, 'the Welsh sign attracted many English people and visitors from Europe.' The 'frightened Englishman' is the great bogeyman in Welsh psychology and it took Welsh nationalists like Myrddin's parents to prove that many English people weren't as ignorant as the majority non-nationalists presumed they were. For the 'frightened Englishman' is really the shadow of the 'scared, and scarred, Welshman'. What was at the root of this Cold War era attitude towards the Welsh language?

This peculiar attitude has to do with the systematic way Welsh was closed out of the world of business, and how the Welsh themselves then chose to cut off their language from the business world too.

It's long been argued that the Welsh language wasn't compatible with commerce and town life. As Adam Price said in his brave lecture, 'Wales: England's First Colony' to the Institute of Welsh Politics at Aberystwyth in November 2009, the Welsh were 'confined to the *favelas* of medieval Wales on the margins of town or in the rural uplands.' This psychology stayed with them and became associated with the Welsh language.

For instance, Cydweli, created in the 1100s, had English, French or Flemish burgesses – but no Welsh (or *forinseci* – yes, 'foreigners') – the Welsh were literally foreigners in their own land. Towns like Carmarthen, Montgomery and Aberystwyth in the Middle Ages were sites of growth for a nascent property-owning English merchant class, but the Welsh became outcasts. In reaction to Llywelyn Bren's revolt of 1294, Edward I banned Welshmen from holding land in borough towns. Punitive Laws in the wake of the Glyndŵr Rebellion decreed in 1401 that no Welshman was to enjoy the privilege of burgess status (an absolute prohibition traditionally reserved for the Jews).

Almost a century and a half after Glyndŵr's uprising, Henry VIII pressed through the Laws of Wales of 1536 and 42. These laws are sometimes grandly named the Acts of Union. The term was coined in 1901 by O. M. Edwards MP for Meirionnydd. I don't think the year is a coincidence. Maybe in the centenary of Ireland's 'Act of Union' and in an echo of Scotland's famous Act, OM tried to give some status to Wales as a constituent nation in the British Isles. He did this by elevating a law into an 'Act' whose declared intention was "utterly to extirpe alle and singular sinister usages and customs" belonging to Wales. Yes, the Welsh, especially the *crachach* (nobility), were glad to be relieved of the punitive laws from Glyndŵr's time – but it came as a cost.

Section XXVI of the 1542 Law states: 'That all Mayors, Bailiffs and Head Officers of Corporate Towns in Wales ... always they follow the Course, Trade and Fashion of the Laws and Customs of the Realm of England, and not of any Welsh Laws or Customs.'

The Welsh became a part of a larger common market, and just like our present European common market were glad of the free movement of produce even if it meant 'standardising' or 'enforcing' common rules . However, unlike the present

European market, the Laws of Wales stipulated that to be successful the Welsh would have to change their language and culture. Unlike the Basques who were allowed to keep their *Fueros* (laws) when they were submerged into the Spanish state, the Welsh lost everything. The Fueros which the Basques kept so jealously have allowed them to keep all their taxes and decide how much is given to Madrid. It's no coincidence, then, that the Basque lands are among the richest and most mercantile in Spain . . . unlike Wales in the UK.

These Laws of Wales were kept on the statute books for centuries. The Laws passed in 1536 were not repealed until 21 December 1993; and the Laws passed in 1543 were repealed on 3 January 1995.

It's undeniable that use of the English language would have spread through Wales and especially in association with commerce, but there was no reason why this couldn't have gone hand in hand with the continuation, if not the flourishing, of the Welsh language. Speakers of all small-language communities understand the need to be bi- or trilingual. But the nature of Wales's relationship with the British state was a colonised one. The 1847 Report into Education was still alive in the macintosh-wearing, chapel-going Llanrwst of the 1950s. Many people, Welsh-speakers as much as anyone, still accepted its view that 'the Welsh language is a vast drawback to Wales, and a manifold barrier to the moral progress and commercial prosperity of the people. It is not easy to over-estimate its evil effects'.

The reaction to Myrddin ap Dafydd's family setting up the first designated Welsh-language book shop gives an insight into the mentality of the age. You were as likely to see Welsh used commercially then as you are today of seeing Zulu, Wolof or Quechua on the shop fronts of South Africa, Senegal or Peru – and for the same reasons. There's enough there to fill several hours in the psychiatrist's chair. And in fact, the Welsh condition has filled hours at Dr Dilys Davies's psychiatrist's couch at Guy's Hospital.

The two old women's *Schadenfreude* at their assumed failure of Arianwen Parri's new venture because it used 'too much Welsh' was what Adam Price MP calls a 'sociological equivalent of Stockholm syndrome' or what experts like Frantz Fanon of Martinique called 'adhesion' to the dominator. For one way of overcoming the feeling of powerlessness that flows from being dominated is to identify with the dominator – sometimes even unconsciously.

Dilys Davies has called this a form of 'cultural autism' and drawn analogies with child sexual abuse which, for all its pervasiveness, was once met by a wall of silence. Colonisation is Wales's 'dangerous idea', a 'dirty little secret', a 'painful memory' that has to be repressed. In this respect, it's not difficult to see why being Welsh nationalist, or 'Welsh nash' as it was called, was such a scorned position to take. It put you literally, and with all puns intended, 'beyond the Pale'. For every nation's struggle for status or independence begins with a civil war.

Today there are some fifty 'Siopau Llyfrau Cymraeg' across Wales and about 1,100 books are published annually in Wales, about half of them in Welsh. This compares with some 1,500 annually in Icelandic or 1,700 in Estonian. The small business revolution Arianwen Parri began in Llanrwst has spread across Wales and clawed away at some of the cringe the Welsh felt when their own language was used publically. It has also help sustain an indigenous Welsh industry whose annual turnover is around £10m. Arianwen and Dafydd Parri not only sold books, they sold an idea. That idea turned on its head centuries of economic assumptions and prejudice and made Wales, and them, richer for it.

Cambria, volume 12, number 1, August-September 2010

Cymru Fydd – Wales of the future

This was something of an intellectual puzzle I set myself, but also a subject long (and deliberately) neglected by Plaid Cymru. When I heard the BBC presenter David Williams, ask Bethan Jenkins, 'How many aircraft carriers would an independent Wales have?' it was a question I just couldn't get out of my head. Like many people I have mixed feelings towards the military. As a young teenager I was a member of the Air Cadets at Gabalfa barracks near my home in Cardiff. I joined because my father had been a member as a young boy, and I wanted a chance to fly. I quite enjoyed it but couldn't take the oath of allegiance to the Queen. My grandfather's uncle, John Jobbins of Pontypool, fought with the South Wales Borderers in the Zulu Wars and came back alive. But then, I'm on the side of the Zulus, not the Welshmen. Yet when I was Mayor of Aberystwyth I would regularly meet the veterans during Remembrance service and other events and always enjoyed talking to the 'old boys'.

So, my feelings towards the military are mixed. I've never been an advocate of neutrality, as it means you expect somebody else to do your fighting for you. Nor do I wish to see Welsh men and women fighting the wars of a dying empire. However, the most surprising aspect of my research was that Wales could have a fully functioning military force at a cost similar, if not smaller, to one we pay for today to the British exchequer.

How Many Aircraft Carriers?

It was the combination of two interviews, one on television in English, the other on radio in Welsh which started me thinking. David Williams, *Dragon's Eye*'s firm but fair presenter, asked Plaid candidate Bethan Jenkins the rather idiosyncratic question: 'How many aircraft carriers would an independent Wales have?' A few months later another BBC interviewer, Radio Cymru's Gwilym Owen, questioned

Plaid's President, Dafydd Iwan, about the rôle of the military in an independent Wales. And whilst Dafydd Iwan was perfectly right to say it wasn't the most pressing of issues at the forthcoming Assembly elections, Gwilym was right to press him about a subject which, it seemed, Plaid Cymru had not thought out at all.

Now, I'm not a defence expert. In fact, I quietly mutter tame Welsh curses when I see that the history section in any shop has been colonised by the soft-porn of historical studies, Military History. My mutterings increase as I notice that once again half of that space is a victim to Second World War *Lebensraum*, exiling more interesting periods, like Europe after the fall of Rome, or Eastern Europe post 1848, to a distant *Reichsprotektorat* next to the nervous twitchings of the Self-Help shelf.

So, as a military, sorry, philosophical exercise, I've tried, with the help of that nice Mr. Wikipedia, to answer the questions Plaid candidates and leaders seem not to think important enough to ask: 'How many aircraft carriers would an independent Wales have?'

Plaid bury their head about this issue, because of their pacifism and also a fear that their political opponents would ridicule it – the 'Plaid would spend £20billion on a Welsh army (ha, ha, ha) not on hospitals' line. Plaid's pacifism partly stems, then, from the need to pacify opponents and distance itself historically from the nationalism of Sinn Féin/IRA. It's also nationalism by proxy. Take the Falklands' Conflict as one example. Plaid could have been straight and said the UK had a right to retake the Falklands by armed force, as a part of her territory had been invaded (by a military junta), but that as Welsh nationalists they believed that this is a war Welsh men and women had no reason to be part of. Instead, Plaid took the 'they should talk and talk . . . and then go for a cup of tea' line. Plaid use the tired stock line that 'war doesn't achieve anything', when in fact war does achieve things – which is, of course, precisely why people do it.

Plaid, could, of course, were it more confident of itself, accuse its opponents of hypocrisy, celebrating Welsh bravery when Welsh men fight under the Union Jack but ridiculing Welsh bravery were they to fight under the Red Dragon. Or it could say that having an independent Welsh military would give the Welsh electorate the choice of which wars Wales wishes to fight and which it doesn't – Suez, Falklands, Iraq spring to mind, to name just a few.

Of course, Plaid could just continue to take its present ersatz-pacifist stance, the stand which made Bethan Jenkins's answer go AWOL when interviewed on *Dragon's Eye*. She couldn't answer the question not because she isn't intelligent, but more pertinently because she lacked the experience in discussing the matter. It's not Bethan's problem entirely, either, because Plaid and its left-wingers have spent the last five years discussing the military in Iraq but haven't spent five minutes discussing what the military capabilities of an independent Wales might be.

Plaid can't pontificate about international issues without coming clean to the public about what Wales's rôle in world affairs would be, post-independence, and how Wales would defend its borders.

There are three simple questions with three comparatively simple answers:

1. What would an independent Wales do with the existing military bases and regiments in Wales?
2. Would it have an armed force and how much would it cost?
3. Would Wales still be part of NATO?

The answer to the first question is yes, a Welsh state would presumably keep the existing structure and infrastructure, but it would come under Welsh control. This would require a bigger change in attitude than anything else. That's not to belittle a totally new change of command, philosophy and war aims. But it's not rocket science either. Armies continuously go through revision and reorganisation. The British Army itself published *Delivering Security in a Changing World* (in 2004) which was itself built on 1998's *Strategic Defence Review*. Bringing the military in Wales under a Welsh chain of command and Chief of Staff would be just another revision and reorganisation in the history of the military of Wales. And heavens, if it couldn't cope with that, then what possible confidence would the Welsh public have in the military defending Welsh interests and sovereignty?

Since the military structure in Wales is minimal, independence would, by all accounts, mean a need to strengthen its fabric rather than diminish it. At present there is no naval facility here, and Wales is used as not much more than a training ground. If the new facility is opened in St Athan I see no difficulty in taking one of three (or a combination of three) options: a) keep the facility as an international training facility for friendly forces; b) develop St Athan as the centre for a Welsh military HQ, combining ground, air and naval command (St Athan is about five miles from Barry docks and 15 miles from Cardiff). The third option, or an added option, would be to lease the facility out to another country, as Iceland does at Keflavik to NATO, or as the Russian navy still does with some ports in Ukraine. Wales could even decide to go under joint command with London – as the Belgians and French proposed (but failed to implement) in the 1930s.

And so on to the second question – would Wales have its own armed forces, and if so, how much would that cost?

Wales could, of course, choose to be unique and make a virtue of being a state with no monopoly of terror over its land. By doing so it would be the only state (excluding the microstates) not to have a force other than the police to defend and promote the democratic will of its elected politicians.

This could lead to four scenarios – the state is open to internal (armed) forces which could destabilise the whole, making it a failed state like Somalia. Part of the state's territory could be beyond its control – the UK's lack of control over South Armagh during the Troubles, parts of Columbia, Georgia, Azerbaijan, Sri Lanka today (2007). A state could keep its territory intact, but a sector of the state's workings is beyond the state's control – vide corruption and mafia in many East European states or even Italy. Having no armed force also means, quite obviously, that the state could be destabilised or conquered by another state.

Now all the above scenarios are unlikely in the current climate (as is independence), but a politician's and a political party's job is to prepare for unlikely situations. Our low birth-rate will create a need for outside labour which may (or may not) cause internal tensions; conflicts could arise over resources like water; what are the implications of the rise in Chinese power? Who knows – as late as 1987 nobody in the intelligence service foresaw the USSR collapsing in 1991, and who could have guessed that English-born Muslims would bomb London buses? The difficulty with not having a military capability is that to build one from scratch would be very difficult and expensive, and in the time it would take, it could spell disaster for the state. In many respects the debate for an independent military capability is like that for sustaining an agricultural sector – things may be good today, and it may well be more cost-effective today to forfeit parts of the agricultural sector, but what of tomorrow?

How much will an independent Welsh military cost? How long is a piece of string? How much will the military of the UK cost in ten or fifteen years' time? It necessarily depends which party is in power and what the circumstances are. But, let's take as a guide, the military spend of other states of similar size and economic and political situation.

The Republic of Ireland, with a population a little over a million more than Wales, spends about £700m on its defence, that's 0.7 of its GDP. Its active force of 10,500 is divided into the Army (8,000), Air Corp and Naval Service.

Slovenia, with a population of 2 million (a million less than Wales), has a military budget is some £270m or 1.7 per cent of its GDP. Slovenia is a NATO member and has about 7,500 officers and some 35,000 personnel – a high number partly because of its previous fragile geo-political situation and the resultant conscription, which came to end only in 2004. Its military is mostly infantry, but it also has a small air force and naval unit. Slovene forces have served in Bosnia, Kosovo, Iraq, Cyprus and the Golan.

So in the light of these examples, how much would an independent Welsh military cost? Again, this depends on what a Welsh government might believe its priorities were at the time. But let's say that Welsh GDP is 4 per cent of the UK's. If the UK's armed forces expenditure in 2006–07 was £34.5bn, then the spend of an independent Welsh military (keeping UK levels of 2.2 per cent) of the state's GDP would be £720m. Now, the UK has major international commitments, partly, I believe, because were the UK to stop being a significant military force, an important plank of the very raison d'être of the UK would fall – something the ruling elite (and, from an emotional standpoint, ordinary people) would not wish to see. This is because the military forms such an integral part of British identity. In fact, without a strong military, people would be tempted to ask what the point of Britain was. What could it do that its constituent nations on their own couldn't?

What if Wales were to take a middle ground approach

between Ireland's 0.7 per cent of GDP and Slovenia's 1.7 per cent? In 2005 Wales's GDP was £35bn, that's almost exactly the same amount as the UK's Defence Budget. In keeping with its size and military legacy, then, let's say 1.5 per cent of Welsh GDP at 2005 levels would give the military a budget of £525m, which would mean a budget less than that of Ireland but more than that of Slovenia.

One imagines the Welsh armed forces would be about 8,000 strong, comprised predominantly of infantry but with an air and naval service more in keeping with Ireland's than Slovenia's (Slovenia has only 16 miles of coastline). Would there be an aircraft carrier? Well, let's come to that in a minute. A Welsh navy would, for obvious reasons, be smaller than Ireland's, but would need to be able to protect our ports, Holyhead, Fishguard and the increasingly important Milford Haven.

And so to our last question. Would an independent Wales be a member of NATO? Again, this assumes there will still be a NATO when Wales achieves independence. Let's assume there is, which would offer us the three options open to any state, the three 'Ns' – Neutrality, Non-alignment, and NATO.

Neutrality generally seems to have proved the favourite option of Plaid rank and file. That's not surprising: the party was formed in 1925 partly as a reaction to the pointless horror of the Great War and a strong desire that Wales would let 'English men fight English wars'. But there are problems with neutrality. It can sound high-minded and moral, but that depends if we believe a conflict with a bully can be satisfactorily solved by a candle-lit vigil, followed by a poetry recital and a question-and-answer session on Waldo Williams's iconic *Mewn Dau Cae*. It's all very well being moral and neutral if your conscience, like that of the Swedes and the Irish, allows you to believe the sons of other nations should defend you from Nazis. But there's not much point being neutral when you're in a minority of one. Now, I could be fighting the 'last war', in that a land war in Europe is unlikely and the need for traditional infantry divisions is superfluous, but that doesn't diminish the need for a military capability. Unfortunately, Plaid's pseudo-neutrality is, more often than not, seen as a cheap piece of Pavlovian positioning against whatever government is in power in London.

Non-alignment is also popular in Plaid, again for obvious reasons. But non-alignment has proved to be a *Star Wars*-style bar of odd-balls: a carnival of dictators and dreamers as ineffective as it was diverse. The European Union may develop into a military alliance, but that seems unlikely as it would undermine NATO. The EU was worse than useless during the Bosnian war, and in any case who would trust an alliance with France and with its ego as a leading player?

The last option is NATO. This would be my preferred option: not because it's perfect but because it has strength – which is the whole point of an alliance. Who knows how Putin's Russia will develop? When I visited in 2005, for instance, every one of the Russians I spoke to believed there would be a dictatorship in five years' time. It's all very well criticising the USA, but I'd prefer Uncle Sam, even under George Bush, than Russia under Putin, or China, with a population of a billion plus, under any leader. So, in my view, an independent Wales should stay in NATO. But then, again, this is a decision which need not be taken now, but could be left to a referendum, in the same way as any question about the rôle of the House of Windsor as head of state would be solved.

The three questions raise many points and many answers. The next time Gwilym Owen or David Williams ask questions on the rôle of the military in an independent Wales, Plaid candidates need to have some answers with coherent philosophical guidelines. Having no military policy – or worse, saying that an independent Wales would have no military at all – is like saying that it wouldn't have any schools or hospitals either.

So, let's return to David Williams's aircraft carrier conundrum. Well, again it depends how a particular government prioritises its spending, but let's put it like this: aircraft carriers are expensive. The Chinese are currently commissioning one for $362m, which would be about half the Welsh Military's annual budget and the US Navy's Nimitz class carrier costs a staggering $4.5 billion. There are only ten states world-wide with aircraft carriers – and so to answer David Williams's question, no, it's not likely Wales would have any at all.

So, to conclude. The more one looks at the facts rather than the clichés and prejudices, the idea of a Welsh independent military force is not only possible, it's actually the most sensible and a cost-effective option.

Look, here are four things to keep in mind.

Wales could have a viable defence force, in line with other forces either of neutral states or NATO members for a smaller percentage of our GNP than our contribution to the UK force.

Furthermore, without the UK's delusions of grandeur and supposedly 'special relationship' a Welsh force would not be involved in so many military conflicts that are both expensive in terms of costs and lives. A Welsh defence ministry could opt out of the expensive contribution towards the re-commissioning of nuclear Trident submarines or may wish to pool its military contribution and capability – on its own terms.

An independent Welsh force would not be starting from scratch either. Not only would it build on centuries of Welsh military knowledge and pride, but under the Vienna Convention on Successor States 1983, Wales, as a successor state to the UK following independence, would be entitled to its corresponding percentage of moveable assets (tanks, aeroplanes, ammunition) and immovable assets (military bases etc).

That means, as Welsh taxpayers have contributed to the UK's military expenditure then some 4 per cent of those military assets would come under Welsh control. For instance, the Royal Navy in 2007 consists of eighty-eight vessels (including one aircraft carrier in reserve). The independence settlement may mean that Wales would get three or four vessels ... or even, horse-bargain and go for the Royal Navy's aircraft carrier, to answer David William's question. The same principle would apply to the air service and army.

Another more elusive but no less important point is that of Welsh prestige. For the first time since the days of Glyndŵr and the Age of the Princes in the twelfth and thirteenth centuries, an ambitious soldier could climb to the top of the armed service within Wales, becoming Chief of Defence Staff without leaving his or her homeland or having a conflict of loyalty. This would be a badge of a 'proper country' – a country that can offer its citizens the broadest possible careers within its borders, culture and principles.

Welsh identity would not be confined to one 'accepted' notion of Welshness but would encompass all aspects of Welsh expression and ambition. For the first time in centuries, Welsh men and women of all ethnic and racial backgrounds would fight Welsh wars on Welsh terms as Welshmen under a Welsh Chief of Defence Staff. There's the incalculable moral and psychological effect of seeing Wales and Welshness not as badges of a weak, defeated nation, but as a nation at arms, a nation, which, if need be, could defend itself – a nation which would deserve to have the Red Dragon as its symbol.

Were the Welsh language to be employed as a practical part to the force (as a some-time medium of instruction, let's say), the effect would be as astounding. For a language unaccustomed to such a setting it would be as liberating for the language as for the Shettle Jews seeing a Jew on horseback. The language of sedate eisteddfodau worthies and good little children would have a renewed muscular strength that it has largely lost with the demise of the heavy-industry Welsh-speaking working class. The whole effect of an independent Welsh force would lead Welsh political and cultural identity into a new field. No more a nation chasing hand-outs but a nation of diplomacy; no more the '*ci rhech*' (lap-dog) yearning for recognition, but a moral nation ready to make its own moral commitments.

Plaid needs to decide if it really is a pacifist party, and if so, put it to a vote at its conference. If it is not a pacifist party, it needs to discuss the implications of independence on the military, so that its own candidates don't go into the firing line of any future election with absolutely no intellectual defence whatsoever. Having your own military capability does not make a nation-state into a warmonger. It means that the state can choose which wars it wishes to fight – and which ones it doesn't. While Wales does not have its own military, answerable to Welsh priorities, Alun Rees' words about the 'Taffy' at the end of his poem 'Taffy was a Welshman, Taffy was a clown' will always ring true:

> He's fought the wide world over,
> He's given blood and bone.
> He's fought for every bloody cause,
> Except his bloody own.[3]

Cambria, volume 8, number 6, February-March 2007

---

[3] Alun Rees, *Yesterday's Tomorrow* (Dinas, Y Lolfa, 2005)

I am at heart a republican, but I also like pageant and history, and more importantly I know that most Welsh people like pageant and history too. To deny that is to deny human nature. So, sometimes, Welsh nationalism has to go with the grain of existing Welsh society, not try and change it.

Moreover, the dull, relentless understatement (usually a mask for not celebrating Welsh identity) just drives me crazy. I blame it on the chapels and the 'poorer than thou' streak in Welsh politics. We'll all be dead some day, so why not have some flamboyance while we're still alive!

I wrote this article to provoke some reaction and to get people thinking. It was sparked by reading an article by the left-wing economist D. J. Davies. About the same time (2005) Norway was celebrating the centenary of its own independence. In any case, it's been a popular article and one I enjoyed writing ... though I don't expect to be knighted soon! (Nor do I want to be!)

Why not a *Welsh* Royal Family?

A recent spate of books has brought out my Cambroindexiphilia like a rash. Yes, I'm one of those men who hover suspiciously in the history department of bookshops, and, having taken a cursory look at the surname of the author, instantly flick to the index to see what references there are to 'Wales' or 'Welsh' in the publication. It's a form of disorder, I know; only one scribbled prescription away from looking for your own name in the index pages of books. But, hey, I'm sure I'm not the only *Cambria* reader who's guilty of this little affliction.

In any case, what with the various TV series with glossy books about royalty and the state opening of the Senedd by the Queen, I've been pondering the rôle of the monarchy in Wales – or, rather, the feasibility of a Welsh monarchy.

I mention my compulsive Cambroindexiphilia because having flicked through various monarch block-busters, one can't but notice that Wales is somewhat lacking in monarchs. And I can't help comparing this with the Scots and feel that this monarchless history undermines our self-confidence as a people. It's one thing to rebel against a historiography of 'Dead Great White Men', but another thing when you don't have many Dead Great White Men to rebel against.

The fact is, people *like* the Monarchy, or, in any case, *a* monarchy. In fact, the poorer they are, the more they like them! Don't get distracted by Welsh left-wing propaganda. For all this macho talk of the Welsh republicans in the Spanish Civil War and the left-wing radical tradition of Wales, on the monarch-ometer it's the Valleys which hit the bell every time. South Wales Labourism's infatuation with royalty is only one notch below the Ulster Unionists'. Whilst the so-called conservative Welsh-speaking *crachach* of the West name their hospitals topographically, the socialists of the Valleys name them after toffs. The royal triangle of Prince Phillip (Llanelli), Princess of Wales (Bridgend) and Prince of Wales (Merthyr Tydfil) is only alleviated from such an uninspiring choice of names by the well-known gag of referring to the Royal Glamorgan Hospital in Llantrisant as the 'Camilla' because it's in between the Prince and Princess of Wales hospitals.

The House of Windsor is as safe as, well, houses. There's no credible challenge to it from the left because royalty today isn't about class: it's about identity. The only challenge to the House therefore comes from a resurgent Welsh and Scottish identity. The WRU's bizarre decision, for instance, to name the new regular rugby fixture between Wales and South Africa the 'Prince William Cup' struck a wrong chord and betrayed a misreading of a less royal-discerning Welsh public mood. It was too late in the day to rename the cup after that great Welshman and human being, Ray Gravell, but if the

WRU members read their own country's history as avidly as they read the annual honours' list they could have named the trophy 'Cwpan David Ivon Jones' in the first place. After all, wouldn't an Aberystwyth-raised Welsh-speaking Unitarian who was one of the founding members of the ANC be a more fitting name for the trophy? I'm not sure if there'll ever be an independent Wales, but I know there will never be a British Republic. I mean, what would be the point of a UK without a King or Queen? Where's the fun in that?

Welsh republicans need to remember then that as Welsh people we've been ruled by monarchs since the days of Cunedda in the fifth century. Wales has been graffitied by names of Welsh and English royalty and it's still going on, thankfully with more prominence to Welsh royalty now. The Princess Gwenllian Society has successfully campaigned to name a summit in Snowdonia, Carnedd Gwenllian, after Llywelyn the Last's daughter. Thanks in no small part to sterling work by unsung patriots like Siân Ifan of the Embassy Glyndŵr, squares and playing fields have been named after Glyndŵr. It's an understandable irony then that when Welsh nationalists assert their republicanism they do so by remembering a prince – Llywelyn, our last prince – at Cilmeri. Royalty is in our blood and can offer a glimpse of a proud Welsh history.

So, what if, in a flight of Iolo Morganwg-style fancy, we offered to create a Welsh monarchy? Impossible? Uncalled for?

Well, there's an interesting article by D. J. Davies which was first published in *Y Faner* in 1953 and then published in English in 1958 in *Towards Welsh Freedom*. D. J. Davies (not to be confused with the other nationalist, the pacifist D. J. Williams) is the little-known brains of Plaid Cymru philosophy. Llandybie–born, DJ was a collier at twelve, became a boxer, American industrialist and First World War pilot, and ended up in Denmark. Impressed by that little country's ability to govern itself, the one-time member of the Independent Labour Party returned to Wales in 1924 a Welsh nationalist. His pamphlets on the economic case for Welsh self-government, co-written by his Irish wife Noëlle, are as fresh now as they where when they were published in 1935 and 1947. DJ's undogmatic, un-statist socialism is the dominant tradition in Plaid's economic and social policy. Saunders Lewis may be better known, and is certainly easier to quote, but it's DJ's policies which are the party's lasting political legacy.

When one considers DJ's background, then his article 'Wales Must Have a King' is all the more surprising. After all, were one to do the blind 'Plaid Challenge' they'd opt for Saunders having written such a piece. In the article DJ recognises that fighting against monarchy is futile, and so suggests that a Welsh monarchy be revived to gain the affection and allegiance of the people of Wales to their own country, not to Britain. DJ suggests elevating an existing Welsh gentry family to become the Royal House and suggests the House of Dinefwr, noting its contribution to Welsh life over centuries and the fact that its scions live in Wales.

However, rather than going for DJ's option I'd like to suggest the 'Norwegian option' only alluded to by DJ: were the UK to face such a political crisis that its very future as a unified state was at stake, then this Norwegian option could be the one on the table. In 1905 the Norwegians voted to declare independence and separate from Sweden – or the 'balkanisation of Scandinavia', as Kim Howells MP would say. It was decided to offer the crown of Norway to the second in line to the Danish throne, Prince Carl. Carl accepted and changed his name to Haakon VII, thereby reviving the historic royal Norwegian legacy which had been broken for six centuries by Danish and Swedish domination.

Could a similar settlement happen in the British Isles were there to be a Scandinavianisation of the UK? It looks very unlikely at the moment – in fact it's not even on the radar, but then, were the political developments to be so seismic, who knows? The Royal family, every royal family, has one allegiance higher than to its country – its own family's continuation – and who wouldn't bet that the Windsors wouldn't take this pragmatic, if not selfish, option?

Were the Scandinavianisation of Britain to happen then one assumes that the King or Queen of the United Kingdom of Great Britain and Northern Ireland would revert to becoming the King or Queen of England. Other siblings could then become heads of state of Scotland or Wales in a new spin on 'divide and rule'. And after all, wouldn't being a head of state – yes, even of Wales – beat being the forever third-in-line? And since kidnapping your brother in a dawn-skirmish and chucking him in a dungeon is no longer politically correct, then it does offer a more sedate way of accommodating sibling rivalry.

Would we take them, for a start? That is the first question. Well, most Welsh nationalists would be circumspect, to say the least. We remember how the present title of Prince of Wales was a dirty trick played by Edward I following our conquest, and how since then the English Royal family and its system have been used as a proxy to undermine Welsh political confidence. A republic, I believe, offers self-respect, but a republic needs to be validated in war to gain true popular affection . . . and I don't want a war. There'd need therefore to be a National Compromise on the issue. The new-look monarch would need to show allegiance to Wales and only Wales; his Welsh would need to be spoken with love and naturalness. But there would be gains to this National Compromise too. A Welsh monarchy, perhaps especially one drawn directly from the House of Windsor, would appeal and give a new voice to a large segment of Welsh society which doesn't feel comfortable with an international Welsh political identity.

I dare say that 'going native' would be a bigger cultural and political change for the royal family than its disbandment. But for most of the world it would be a case of 'change – what change?' Bearing in mind that the present Queen is habitually referred to as the 'Queen of England' and seeing that we already have a 'Prince of Wales' in title at least, it would be *plus ça change.*

The new monarch would need to have a royal Welsh name, say Llywelyn, Owain, Hywel, Rhys, or Gwenllian, Nest, Angharad, Siwan, and in a hat-tip to the Norwegian experience could become Llywelyn III or Owain II as a sign of continuity with a millennium of history. We could dispense with a lot of the work of the Ministry for Silly Walks and create a new more aerodynamic royal code and customs.

This new monarchic set-up would be built on a changing sensibility and appreciation of the rôle of the Welsh monarchy. The work by the sorely-missed Professor R. R. Davies on Glyndŵr and Welsh medieval history; the ground-work pioneered by the Welsh history society, Cofiwn, in the 1980s; today's History Forum for Wales, and the S4C series (and accompanying book in Welsh and English) *Tywysogion* (Princes) have, over the years, opened the door to our own national dignity: an age when Welsh society was whole – a cultural community with 'high', as well as 'low', culture. We once were princes – making our own laws and writing our own international treaties, not just soon-to-be patients defined by our illness. Furthermore, a fully-functioning, fit-for-purpose, truly bilingual Welsh monarchy would elevate Welsh in the eyes of our people to a status it hasn't known since the days of Glyndŵr.

The Welsh cultural community must be able to answer

the aspirations of that community. And whilst a royal head of state (as opposed to a presidential one) negates the aspirations of individuals in that community, it would answer the collective aspiration. It would give us world-wide status, recognition and authority.

In thirty or fifty years time, people will still gossip about the latest royal scandal no matter what the effects of climate change or the country's GNP. Would it not be a small, but decisive victory for Welsh nationality if they gossiped about a Welsh, rather than an anglicised, royal family?

In an age when the old states of Europe are dissolving and the hidden nations raising their heads, the Norwegian option could offer a useful compromise for many. This could certainly be the case for two other European constitutional monarchies with growing calls for independence within their borders: the increasing calls for Flanders to leave Belgium and the Faeroe Islands to leave Denmark.

So back to Wales. I'm no great monarchist. Like so many, by instinct I'm a republican. So, I suppose what I'm saying is that the Welsh state needs to offer its people pageant, glamour, uniforms, symbols, medals, authority and status. With the exception of Iolo's Gorsedd of the Bards, which recognises contributions to Welsh culture, the Welsh state neither thanks nor elevates people's contributions to society and state. Until, therefore, we shatter the axis of Nonconformist dullness and the institutionalised anti-establishmentism of the '68ers', does it come as any surprise that Welsh people invest their aspirations in the English royal family?

Belatedly, and against my natural instincts, I'm coming to believe that Wales will never be truly independent unless it has its own monarchy. Maybe it's time for Wales to get out of the book indexes and start writing its own royal history.

Cambria, volume 9, number 5, January-February 2008

Demography is the mother of all politics, but it's consistently ignored or understated in Welsh political discourse. It's not discussed, of course: not because it's not important, but because it is so important. Really important issues are rarely discussed until the establishment gives in.

The flow of young people from Wales is something which really breaks my heart. My heart sinks when I hear a proud parent proclaim that their Dafydd or Sarah is now doing very well in Manchester or London. England, it seems, is now full of little kids with Welsh names given by their patriotic (and maybe slightly guilty) parents.

The Irish have a great narrative of their lost generations, but because Wales is not an island but is part of a big state, our huge human loss is rarely commented on. The financial investment we make in our young people is not half as important as the incalculable cultural and linguistic investment.

Birth-rates in countries across the globe are decreasing. The debate which I hope I raise in the article about retaining people in their homeland will in future become acute, as states (even those who are not so wealthy today) will not be able to be so laissez-faire with their young people.

Dai-aspora

It's probably because I suffer from Selective Ethnocentric Dyslexia that for years I would read and write 'Diaspora' as 'Dai-aspora', blissfully smiling like a pig in dung at the good grace of the Greeks to create a word using the Welsh diminutive of Dafydd to describe a world-wide age-old phenomenon.

I was incorrect, of course, but at the same time possibly not wrong either. After all, isn't every community's Diaspora a special, unique and more wholesome Diaspora than the rest? One community's economic immigrant, under-cutting costs and wages, is another community's heroic, downtrodden worker, finding a better life for himself and family to send much-needed money home to mother and the motherland.

Madog is the alpha of our diaspora, as he left a Wales plagued by civil war and famine in 1170 to discover, luckily, America where, by coincidence, he found many Welsh societies celebrating St David's Day and sharing his name. The Cymmrodorion Society in London played an instrumental part in the founding of many of our national institutions. My guess is that the Welsh language was the largest 'ethnic' language in England until the recent advent of Hindi and Polish-speakers. Even today the Welsh Language Board believes there to be some 150,000 Welsh-speakers in England – a 'Slough-sized' population – albeit dispersed and largely disinterested.

So as we crawl into a century when demography, diaspora and birth-rate will be the bed-rock of politics, maybe now is as good a time as ever to examine the whole idea of a diaspora.

I guess many Welsh people have quite a low estimation of the Welsh diaspora – if they think of it all. Maybe it's coloured by Jac Glan-y-Gors, the eighteenth-century republican from Cerrigydrudion. This sometime tenant of the King's Head pub in Ludgate St, London, penned the famous ballad to the eponymous, treacherous Dic Siôn Dafydd, the fictional Welshman who 'forgot' his mother tongue as soon as he settled in England. The Welsh idiom 'Gorau Cymro, Cymro oddi cartref' (Best Welshman, Welshman away from home) is said more often than not with a sarcastic and knowing smile than as a true compliment. Almost uniquely among the world's diaspora, the Welsh one seems to be less radical and less nationalistic than the folks back home.

Like my fellow *Cambria* columnist, Patrick Thomas, I have an interest in Armenia, whose people, along with the Jews, share the most envious of diasporas – and also for tragic reasons. In the early years of this decade, the Armenian diaspora, for instance, raised $25 million through its annual Thanksgiving Phonathon to finance the building of a 100-mile road in the Armenian enclave of Nagorno-Karabakh – yes a fully-tarmaced, two-lane, dead straight highway – you know, just like the one we don't have linking north and south Wales.

The Welsh diaspora is less impressive but now seems to be somewhat in fashion. Websites such as the www.glaniad.com (Patagonia) and the Wales-Ohio Project wish to archive, digitise and put online the Welsh global experience. There's also been a series of interesting programmes in both Welsh and English about elements of the history of the Welsh diaspora from the American Civil War, our communities in Ohio and of course the Wladfa. As Chief Executive of the bid for .cymru I've witnessed the importance of the Welsh diaspora to the growing success of the bid, and also for creating a world-wide network of societies which gives an international context to our identity.

Even so, I can't help asking if we *should* be creating a culture which elevates the diaspora. It was our good fortune as a nation to have black gold under them thar hills of Glamorgan and Gwent, which meant we emigrated from Bethesda to Merthyr for work rather than to America. Less heroic I know, less newsworthy and less worldwide well-known, but should we measure the success of our culture by the word-recognition of the American on Main Street?

Doesn't a celebration of diaspora lead to a 'they got out of jail' mentality – with Wales being the 'jail'; where being a teacher in Reading is better than being a teacher in Lampeter, or being a merchant banker in the City is better than being a 'lowly' bank manager in Swansea who is nevertheless an important element of the Welsh community, possibly raising the kids to speak Welsh and paying taxes in Wales?

If we celebrate our diaspora, then what right do we have to say that other diasporas should integrate into our society, or rather, where do you draw the line? Maybe with so many people and so many diasporas forming globally we all need to underplay the rôle of the diaspora – including our Welsh one.

So, what is this animal we call a 'Welsh diaspora'? Is there such a thing, or are there just Welsh individuals who live outside Wales? And does it present a problem?

At a glance, the demography of Wales looks quite healthy, with an annual increase in population of some 10,000. But this headline figure masks the true situation, which is more subtle and leaves a little less room for complacency.

According to the Assembly's Statistical Bulletin, from 1975 to 2003 there was an overall net emigration to the rest of the word from Wales of approximately 6,600, which is low and stable. In the decade to 2003, a total of 555,000 emigrated from Wales; 87 per cent of whom moved to another country within the UK, the overwhelming majority to England. Over the same period a total of 631,000 people migrated into Wales, of which 85 per cent were from the rest of the UK. In UK terms this movement of people would correspond to about 11 million moving out and in during the course of a decade. In linguistic terms, were English in the same situation as Welsh, then some 1–2 million English-speakers would have been 'lost', never to be replaced, and the remaining English-speakers would have become a smaller percentage of the population.

According to the Report, with the exception of the south-east region (lowland Gwent, Cardiff and the Vale) a substantial number of those moving in are of retiring age, or approaching retiring age, adding to an already ageing domestic population. So the population isn't growing because of the birth-rate, nor, except in one of Wales's five regions, necessarily because of employment. In brief, there seems to be a straight swap between England and Wales, but with Wales losing between 1–2,000 a year more in the important sixteen to twenty-four age group.

We're familiar with current East European levels of emigration, the effects of which are starting to cause real concern for the governments of countries like Poland and Latvia. But has not the Welsh experience, today and over decades, been just as seismic? The magnitude of the effect of emigration on Wales is either invisible or is ignored. Obviously a section of Welsh society leaving Wales for a job in England is no great move, either in terms of distance nor culture. However, for the Welsh-language, the effect of this movement of people, I would argue, reaches East European levels. This is the 'elephant in the room' as far as language planning is concerned.

On average 19,700 people aged between eighteen and twenty-four left Wales each year between 1999 and 2004 (with, on average, 18,700 moving in). I would guess that most of these are students. It's not as great in number or percentage as the numbers currently leaving East European states, but I'd reckon that this constant movement has been happening for decades in Wales and could continue, whereas the emigration from Latvia or Poland is a temporary one and will soon come to an end as life and jobs improve there. In that respect, the haemorrhaging of Welsh talent (and culture and language) is as acute in Wales as it is for East European countries, if not more. One of the main structural reasons for this haemorrhaging is particular to Wales – higher education – which I'll come to later.

Just like the demographic graphs for Latvia, the graphs look pretty grim for the Welsh-language community. A Welsh Language Board Statistical Trends presentation in 2004 estimated that within the Welsh-speaking community the number of deaths (6,500) and emigration to England (5,200) outran the number of children born to Welsh-speaking homes or raised Welsh-speaking, plus immigration of children into Wales (from England, mostly) by 3,000. These aren't precise figures and are maybe skewed towards the more western, Welsh-speaking parts of Wales to the detriment of the east. Having said that, the presentation calculated that the Welsh-language community is running at a deficit of 3,000 a year. On top of that is a below-average replacement birth-rate, with Ceredigion as the lowest in the UK.

So: death, 'below replacement' birth-rate, and a growing diaspora are haemorrhaging away the life of community – exactly as is happening to Latvia – but without the Welsh language having the same status as Latvian, and with a large number of people moving in. Were Wales an island or a nation-state this would be a subject of newspaper headlines, university papers and political debate. As it stands, it's barely noticed or even mentioned.

These are still early days in terms of measuring specific Welsh demography and so there is much more we need to learn, but Hywel Jones, Statistician at the Welsh Language Board, estimates that some 17 per cent of Welsh-speakers live outside Wales. According to the 1991 census, 21.8 per cent of those born in Wales (of whatever age and background) now live in England. This isn't an annual figure, of course, but even so it sounds alarmingly large enough to me. This means that if one were to consider a typical Welsh school year, it may reasonably be expected that 1 in 5 of those children will have left Wales after twenty or thirty years.

Not that emigration from Wales is new. Between 1925 and 1939 Wales lost 390,000 people, and its population did not regain the 1925 level until 1973. But whereas the closure of the mines led many to leave Wales in the past, we're starting to wake up to another cause now – higher education. This is one challenge Eastern Europe won't have to contend with to such an extent.

Brain-drain is a concern for all communities, including the British community, which frets that the best are tempted away by the USA. Within the UK, Ulster Protestants, for instance, are concerned about the number of Northern Irish students choosing to study in Scotland. Whilst this has been an historic concern, the 'threat' is greater now than ever. It's one thing when only some 6 per cent of the population entered university, as in the 1960s, but it's a whole new ball-game when 40 per cent do so, as is the case now. It's a complicated area as the student community is by its very nature fluid, and Wales gains economically from the post-graduates who stay here. But for anyone interested in the continuation of the Welsh language it's important to understand what's happening.

As it is, the whole issue is being swept under the carpet. No, I'm wrong – it's worse than that. During the first Assembly in 2001, Cynog Dafis AM, Chair of the Education Committee, raised the possibility of conducting research to find out how many young people decided to follow university courses in England and what proportion returned to Wales. Incredibly, this caused a massive outpouring of misunderstanding or misquotation and, certainly, mischief. Among the many academics who gave presentations to the committee was the eminent lecturer, Dafydd Glyn Jones, a man who has given decades of service to academia, lecturing both on campuses and, in his spare time, in village halls. Dafydd Glyn made the fatal mistake, in his presentation to

200

the committee, of a) wishing to see Welsh students study in Wales and thus help build a strong confident nation, and b) having a sense of irony. Unfortunately for Dafydd Glyn, Labour AMs on the committee had no sense of irony and seemed unconcerned by the Welsh brain-drain from Wales. The AM for Merthyr, Huw Lewis, attempted to censure Dafydd Glyn Jones's comments as supposedly 'racist'.

The Labour party group refused to consider any recognition of the need to attract more Welsh students to study in Wales. Cynog Dafis's motion 'that stemming the flow of talented young people from Wales to receive their Higher Education should be recognised as a problem, and that Higher Education Funding Council for Wales, in cooperation with others, are to draw a strategy to promote a substantial percentage of Welsh students to receive their education in Wales' was defeated. Yes – a *Welsh Assembly education committee* turned down the promotion of Welsh colleges to Welsh students! Little wonder our young people leave Wales if some of our politicians don't think it's worth studying here,

Thankfully, the rather touchy reaction to Cynog Dafis's sensible concern has calmed down a little since then, and he has been partly vindicated. The decision to offer financial breaks to Welsh students who study within Wales has led (by default rather than desire) to an increase in students staying in Wales – and hey, they've got no scars! Dafydd Glyn's good name has also been restored and his dream of a Welsh language Federal College (a notion to which some on the committee were also hostile, no doubt on grounds of 'diversity' and 'equality') vindicated with, the Assembly government now committed to 'establish a Welsh-medium Higher Education Network – the Federal College – in order to ensure Welsh-medium provision in our universities'.

No state, nor any parent for that matter, has the right to

stop an individual leaving a community – for either study or work. But a community, in the form of a state, most definitely has an obligation to work creatively to make its country as attractive as possible to its people so that they will wish either to stay or return to it – yes, to undermine 'diasporism'. It also has a moral obligation to foster the unique culture and language of that state or else it will lose the moral reason for its existence. This all hinges on a basic tenet: do the state's politicians think that the cultural and linguistic existence of that state is something worth continuing in the first place? Maybe, many in the Labour party didn't believe it in 2001.

Demography – the movement of peoples, and its consequences – will be the mother of the politics of the twenty-first century, yet it is a subject which is given scant attention. Why do we talk of a 'sustainable environment' but not a 'sustainable population'? Welsh tax-payers invest in the nursery, primary and comprehensive education of our children, to the tune of an estimated £100,000 for each and every one, not to mention the equally important emotional – and for many of us, linguistic and cultural – investment. As things stand, from a tax-payer's perspective we may as well cut out the middle man and send our children straight from the maternity ward to Manchester, London or Bristol with a cheque for £100,000 pinned to their nappies.

States and communities will have to live with the reality that their citizens have the choice where they wish to spend their adulthood. Building dykes and walls won't work, nor should it. But having a totally laisser-faire attitude to the loss of its people, as Wales has at present, isn't sustainable in the long term for the survival of a small and comparatively weak linguistic and cultural community like that of Welsh-speaking Wales and, I dare say, parts of Eastern Europe and Africa.

For me, one of the strongest arguments for Welsh independence is that it will break the 'glass ceiling' of job opportunities which don't, and can't, exist in Wales under the present arrangement: prestigious jobs in high government, a Foreign Office for instance, the military, the financial sector, jobs at the head of important organisations with an international dimension, jobs in senior management. Lack of political ambition for Wales as a nation means that a section of our talented and ambitious people will always leave. Wales has to be a diverse, multi-ethnic, interesting, safe – and Welsh – place to live. This is no mean feat in an age where people can choose to live in different countries for reasons such as wanting a year-round sun-tan, winter skiing, sexuality, taxation or religion.

The more I think about it, the more I believe that in twenty years time our almost cavalier attitude to population movement will seem as irresponsible and short-term as the throw-away unsustainable environmental policies of the 1970s do today.

In states with 'below replacement' birth rates, governments will need to create ways to keep their young people – the very people in which they have invested culturally and financially so greatly – as well as attract the best from outside. Tax-breaks may be used to reward those who stay or return, and Wales will need to offer a full range of careers from the very highest in government to the latest in technology. One thing's for sure: raising millions of dollars to build roads in far-off homelands or even holding marches for patron saints in foreign cities won't be seen as signs of success – but of failure.

Cambria, volume 9, number 3, September-October 2007

The economic poverty of Wales is as nothing compared to the poverty of ambition many people have for Wales. If Wales, and Welshness, isn't intellectually exciting, and doesn't offer people interesting career paths, then it's no wonder people leave our land and others have never heard of it.

For me, the Welsh experience is a holistic one. It encapsulates a vision for Wales and an international context to our identity which is both rewarding and interesting. Not to develop an independent Welsh foreign policy is to relegate Welsh aspirations to a lower division and to forfeit a Welsh world view with its own morality and priorities. It relegates Wales and Welshness to a child-like identity, one which doesn't 'trouble it's pretty little head' with 'grown-up' ideas.

Having been born in Zambia and with a great interest in European affairs and history, a Welsh foreign policy is a natural dimension to my identity. When I came across the ideas of the Polish leader, Piłsudski, it seemed to me an obvious template for Wales to follow, and one which, instinctively, so many individuals and institutions already do.

Time to start thinking about Welsh Foreign Policy

The 2008 Olympic Games in Beijing underlined Wales's invisibility on the world stage. Lumped with Tibet and other submerged nations, our flag banned, Wales was air-brushed from the world map. It seems that for Wales to be recognised as an Olympic country it would need to be a sovereign state. But, apart from fielding her own team at the Olympic games how else would a sovereign Wales wish to be represented internationally and, to take it a step further, what kind of foreign policy would she follow?

Poland, like Wales, is a country which has consistently been made invisible in world atlases. The great Polish interwar leader, Józef Piłsudski, formulated a foreign policy doctrine before the outbreak of the First World War which, he believed, would gain Poland's sovereignty, secure her borders and enhance her leading position in Eastern Europe. I'd like to suggest we in Wales follow it.

The doctrine included two complementary strands. One was Międzymorze, often translated as 'Intermarium' (between the seas i.e. Baltic and Black). It meant the creation of a federation of Central and Eastern European countries from Finland and Estonia down to Yugoslavia. The other was Prometeizm ('Prometheism'). Prometheism's aim was to weaken the Russian empire and its successor, the Soviet Union, by supporting the independence movements of the major non-Russian peoples that lived within her borders. Piłsudski had the foresight to see that a sovereign Poland could only survive in a mosaic of other 'new' sovereign states. This Big Idea continues today and is the moral guideline for successive Polish governments. It's the reason Poland was a strong supporter for the Ukrainian Orange Revolution in 2006; of Georgia during the 2008 war; and of the Belorussian language and pro-democracy activists.

In the same way Wales cannot survive and will not exist (except in an ethnic form) if it is part of a Western Europe of a few *ancien regime* 'nation' states. It is only with the weakening of these centralised states and the strengthening through a strategy of our Intermarium (from the Celtic to the Mediterranean Sea) of smaller nations from Scotland to Catalonia that Wales can flourish.

How would the doctrine advance Wales's interests in concrete policy areas?

Like all foreign doctrines its first call is to defend and promote Wales's economic and cultural interests. These economic interests include Welsh produce and services and increasingly Welsh energy and water. Wales is already a net exporter of electricity and the Valleys are sitting on approximately 13 trillion cubic feet of coal-bed methane gas and water will be an invaluable commodity. But economic projects would not be the only concern of a Welsh foreign policy. The morality of the Welsh state is the defence and promotion of the Welsh language and expressions of Welshness in English. The doctrine of Intermarium and Prometheism across Western Europe would give strength and context to this morality in a way which is lacking today. The more power Scotland or Catalonia have, the stronger Wales will also become as the march towards Welsh sovereignty will only happen in a Western-Europe-wide movement.

The existence of a Welsh state is a deeply moral one and the morality of that state calls for its defence. Wales would therefore seek military alliances. NATO, as the biggest and strongest alliance of democratic states, would be the obvious choice. But an independent Wales would have a choice to form its own alliances and fight its own wars and could, for instance, follow the Irish who participate in the Nordic EU Battlegroup.

The Welsh doctrine of Intermarium and Prometheism would welcome the fresh air let into foreign affairs by the disintegration of the old Westphalian consensus of state sovereignty. This doctrine since 1648 has called for the non-interference in the affairs of states and the inviolability of existing borders. The wilting away of this doctrine following the Kosovo war, and unilateral Russian recognition of Abkhazian and South Ossetian independence in 2008, brings with it uncertainty – but also opportunity. It was a doctrine which was habitually ignored when great powers so wished, but was used as a thin excuse when they were called to act on an ethical foreign policy. Why should Wales, with a history as a stateless nation, uphold a doctrine which has consistently ignored the rights of stateless nations? Our foreign policy will be Wilsonian in outlook and will recognise the rights of nations as well as states – which aren't always the same nor part of the same 'integral' borders. But in a post-Westphalian theatre, with pressures of demography and resources, Wales will recognise the need for strong alliances in a world where might will be right.

Wales has a golden opportunity to be a world leader. Intermarium and Prometheism give us the guidelines. Whilst all western countries place human rights (or even women's and religious rights) at the top of their foreign policy agenda, none openly defines human rights as including linguistic rights. Wales could lead the way in this field of international law, a field, as the barrister, Gwion Lewis notes in his excellent pamphlet *Hawl i'r Gymraeg* (Y Lolfa, 2008), that is lacking in recognition but which is set to grow in prominence. On confident intellectual ground the Welsh Minister for Culture would, for instance, raise concerns with the French Government and L'Académie Française over their lack of recognition and respect for Breton linguistic rights in the recent debate in the French Assembly on an amended French constitution. After all, this is what the Estonian government does time after time in respect of their related languages, like Mari (a Finno-Ugric language spoken by some 643,000 people) stranded in the Russian Federation. As the Estonians understand, an attack on linguistic rights of one small language is an attack on all small languages.

As Intermarium and Prometheism are the only intellectual credible and logical strategies for a Welsh Foreign Policy, how will they be built?

Wales has a strong and proud history of international

sporting relationships on which to build, as well as long-standing membership of many international bodies in its own right, from the Commonwealth to the Anglican Communion. There are also now (2008) thirty-one foreign consulates based in Cardiff from countries as diverse as Brazil to Kazakhstan.

Since the opening of the Assembly in 1999, other steps have also been taken – steps which are by the way, intentionally or unintentionally, Intermarian. The government has signed several Memoranda of Understanding: with the Breton Regional Council on 16 January 2004, Latvia on 13 May 2004 and the Argentine province of Chubut (which includes the Welsh colony).

Over the years, the Welsh people have also been active internationally in a way that is instinctively Intermarian. This has manifest itself in the formation of such bodies as Cymdeithas Cymru-Llydaw (Wales-Brittany Society), participation in the Interceltic Festival or the Celtic League, and in other more structured settings due to the need for Wales to form alliances. This has led to the formation of the Celtic Film and Television Festival or the Welsh Language Board's membership of the EU's Network for Promoting Linguistic Diversity (launched in June 2008).

The visit by Westminster's Welsh Affairs Committee to the Basque Country and Catalonia to study 'Globalisation and its Impact on Wales' in April 2008 is a recognition that these strategic international alliances have stepped from the realm of the abstract to mainstream Welsh political discourse.

In a multi-polar world, Wales would naturally take on board a multi-polar identity. Wales may wish to play the Celtic identity; a combined Celtic rugby touring team or fielding a Celtic Cricket Association like the West Indies in the next cricket world cup. Likewise, Wales could instigate a policy of 'country twinning' as it already does to all intents and purposes with the southern African state of Lesotho through Dolen Cymru-Lesotho. In an extended EU it may wish to extend the logic of Intermarium to create a block of small sovereign states within the EU – uniting the peripheries from Estonia across to Scotland and Ireland down to Catalonia over to Kosovo.

But firstly Welsh civic society needs to take Wales seriously. We possess a world-renowned Department for International Politics in Aberystwyth University which has produced no study of any kind on Wales' rôle in the world. It could host a biennial international conference of Wales's strategic interests along the lines of the Königswinter Conferences which are held to develop and enhance Anglo-German relationships.

Implementing a Welsh Foreign Policy Doctrine would mean investing in a foreign presence – an investment which will enhance job prospects and ambitions within Wales. This can be developed immediately building on our existing devolution settlement and foreign offices and need not go as far as full diplomatic relations. These Welsh centres could combine the rôle of bodies such as the German Goethe Instituten or Euskal Extea (Basque House) and be a focus of Welsh culture in foreign cities; a place to learn Welsh, promote Welsh produce in a deli and restaurant, see concerts and even offer accommodation. They would be located in the main *Weltstädter* from Washington DC to Beijing. The cost of a network of Tŷ Cymru? Well, as a guideline, the British Council's 2006–07 funding from the Westminster government was £188m. As a percentage of this according to population, Welsh taxpayers already contribute some £9m. A similar figure for Tŷ Cymru (with added income from sales and events) would offer Wales a bespoke window on to the world which could happen now.

But an independent Wales could go a step better and afford its own Diplomatic Missions. Ireland has seventy-four missions across the world, including fifty-five embassies. This comes at a price of course ... but then, at present, Welsh taxes also go to supporting the UK's Diplomatic Missions – and the UK's foreign wars. The question is, would Wales get a better deal from financing its own Diplomatic Service than from chipping in to the UK one?

Well, the UK's Foreign and Commonwealth Offices's budget is £1.7bn. As an indicator, as percentage of population of the UK, the contribution of Wales to the FCO is about £80m (a little over half the present budget of the Welsh Government's Heritage Ministry – itself one of the smallest departments in WAG). This figure alone would give us a foreign office and diplomatic service of about the same size as Ireland's – some 1,400 members of staff in seventy-four diplomatic missions world-wide. Wales could also pool resources with the other Britannic or EU states. Wales's money would be for the first time spent on a dedicated diplomatic service, working '24/7' for Welsh interests.

Józef Piłsudski's doctrine of Intermarium and Prometheism has served Poland well and given it a moral standing and courage which many states lack and which Wales really needs. When the Olympic games were last held in London in 1908 there was no Polish flag to represent a Polish team. The strategy of Intermarium and Prometheism has helped secure an Olympic team for Poland and for many other formerly stateless nations. The same strategy could gain for Wales and other historic nations full recognition at the Olympics in the future.

Cambria, volume 10, number 3, September–October 2008

One of the scariest songs in the world is John Lennon's 'Imagine'. The line 'imagine there's no country, it isn't hard to do' sends shivers down my spine. Rather than being a peace song for brotherly love and understanding, 'imagine there's no country' is usually the template and intellectual excuse used by large countries to deny rights for smaller nations within their borders. I'd bet more deaths have been inflicted by the governing states insisting on staying 'unified' and suppressing nations wishing to become 'new countries' than there have been by peoples wishing to secede. Imagining 'there's no country' means language death and cultural euthanasia.

During the 1980s and 1990s I would occasionally be challenged by 'progressives' with Lennon singing in their dreamy heads over why I believed Wales should have its own parliament. People would argue that nationalism started wars. They'd always be in favour of 'government closer to the people' except, it seemed, if those people thought of themselves as 'Welsh', or as 'a nation'.

And then, in 1997 Wales voted for our Assembly and our country started to become a state. But then the question I asked myself was, well, if the nation state gets all post-national and doesn't promote the things which make it a nation – like a daily newspaper for the Welsh-speakers – then what's the point of having your own nation-state?

What's the *point* of Wales?

If the historian, Gwyn Alf Williams, famously asked 'When was Wales?' I'd like to ask, 'What's the point of Wales?' That is, why choose to invest effort in furthering Welsh nationality, and why then wish to create a Welsh state?

It's a question I've been pondering for some time. It popped up again during the fall-out over the government's funding (or rather lack of funding) of the proposed Welsh language daily newspaper, *Y Byd*.

Assuming that all people have to live in a state of some sort then the decision has to be made on what criteria should that state be based. We could all live in our own city-state or maybe another entity devoid of the suspected evils of nationality. This, some believe with almost child-like innocence, will immunise us from xenophobia. We could base our state on ideology or religion – communism maybe, Jewish Eruv, Islamic Ummah or be like the Holy Roman Empire – though, I doubt whether non-national states would immunise us from conflict nor injustice. So, why choose a state based on Welsh nationality?

I would argue that the creation of a Welsh state, as opposed to a state based on another identity, gives prestige, status and power to a language which would, otherwise, be totally marginalised. That is, the political and cultural agenda of creating a Welsh state is a vehicle through which to strengthen the Welsh language and culture – it's not an end in itself. The revival of the Welsh language is the moral purpose of Wales. That's the point of prioritising a Welsh nationality rather than a regional, city or British one. In a globalised world, not having a nation state is certain death for 'small' languages – as the leaders of the Tibetan intifada of 2008 understand only too well.

The moral purpose of a state, in the European model at least, isn't to make its citizens wealthy, healthy, happy or fair-minded. Though these attributes are important, they are all attributes which can be given to a population by another state – a conquering state, say, or a more powerful 'paternal' state. No, the moral purpose of a nation, and the only reason for its unique existence, is to promote its unique language and culture. If the state of which that nation is a part doesn't achieve that, then there is no moral purpose to that state.

So, the reason for 'inventing' nationality is to defend and promote a particular language and culture. In fact, the argument in favour of conferring nationality is similar to the one about defence, and includes the same irony which I'd argue should be reversed. It's always tickled me that larger countries are the ones claiming they need a nuclear bomb to 'defend themselves'. But doesn't history teach us that it should be the other way round? Should not Chechnya or Poland have the nuclear bomb rather than Russia; New Caledonia rather than France; Tibet rather than China? Nuclear bombs should be given to countries that really need to defend themselves. Likewise, should not nationality or independence be conferred to communities which need it to strengthen a weak or threatened language rather than to those whose identity is already sufficiently strong: Lakota Indians, Karen or Bretons (or Welsh) rather than USA, Burma, France?

But back to Wales and the cause célèbre of *Y Byd*, the dreamed-of Welsh language daily newspaper which had been led to expect adequate financial support from the Welsh Assembly Government, but which was offered a grant which was simply far too meagre. The whole issue of language and culture in Wales should be put in the context not only of what's possible, but what needs to be done to further the moral purpose of the Welsh state. The defence by the British state of what it sees as its moral purpose should put this, and other decisions by the Welsh Government, in context and, maybe, ask us to frame our whole political argument in a different world view.

The 'moral reason' for the British state is the big question with which the Labour Prime Minister Gordon Brown is grappling today. After a heady series of post-national or anti-national arguments, he's been forced to agree to some old-fashioned criteria which could be summed up as: mother tongue, the military and the monarchy.

What price this 'Britishness'? Well, you could say it includes the lives of forty-eight Welsh Guards. That's how many died on the warship Sir Galahad, in the South Atlantic to defend the Falkland Islands from Argentine control in 1982. Now, unlike many Welsh nationalists, I believe the Falklands War to have been a 'just conflict' as, from a British point of view, a hostile force invaded a part of the national territory. Had the UK not defended that territory then the whole question of the viability of its state would have been brought into question. Thatcher decided she had to fight back. Moreover, Argentina was ruled by a junta which was chucking Good People out of aeroplanes or 'disappearing' them. But that doesn't deny the fact that the Falklands war, more than just a war about oil, or Thatcher's prestige, or a fight against a fascistic junta, was an ethnic war. It was a war by an English-speaking community which didn't want to become a Spanish-speaking community. It was no different in essence to the recent Balkan Wars, First World War, Palestinan Intifada or Glyndŵr's war.

A case could have been made that incorporating the Falkland Islands into Argentina would have improved its economy, health service and education. But that isn't the point of a state. The point of a state is to defend the language indigenous to that state. That and that alone is the moral point of having one's own state.

The actual defence of the English language (but not Welsh) by war is then an integral part of the morality of the British state. But the British state goes yet another step in its moral justification, and that is in its identification with the British military and even the support for extra-territorial wars. These wars can be called 'Crusades', the 'white man's burden', 'just wars' or 'liberal interventionism', but they all add up to what the French would recognise as *la Gloire*. The price of promoting British Gloire? Well, in 2008, the Iraq and Afghanistan wars alone cost £3bn. War, the justification of war, are all essential parts of British moral identity, with the Second World War being in all but name what the Russians would call The Great Patriotic War. For, after all, what's the point of Britain if it doesn't have a military which 'punches above its weight'? So, £3bn is one price for promoting a moral reason for the British state.

What of other costs for promoting this moral purpose? Well there's the British Council with its £500m budget, and the BBC's World Service budget of £250m, both for promoting British culture and the English language – and that's before we mention the Olympic-sized £9bn for the 2012 Olympics. These are all good, valid cultural strategies and show an inherent understanding by the British state of the importance of mother tongue and Gloire. On the other hand, the entire budget of the National Assembly of Wales's Heritage Department for the defence and promotion of our moral purpose is a mere £156m. It's worth keeping these figures in mind when the our politicians and yes, we the public, discuss culture.

Which brings us on to the debate about the funding of *Y Byd*. The sum offered was £200k or, to give some context, 0.2 per cent of S4C's annual budget. Since the inception of the Assembly the prestige of publishing in Wales has increased, but I'm still struck by the discrepancy between money thought acceptable for publishing, compared with what many think is vital for television. Possibly the poverty of our economy is as nothing compared to the poverty of our ambition, and the whole debate about what is 'politically acceptable' in the financing of publishing in Wales needs to be seen in another context.

Many of the arguments against allotting additional money for *Y Byd* centred on the incompatibility of the state funding a daily newspaper. This, of course, is a valid argument, but seems to ignore the fact that in other countries the state does subsidise daily newspapers and press in general. The British state has funded the English-language press in the UK and here in Wales, through laws which first created English-speakers and then English-readers, thus preparing a viable market for the English-language press. The 'Acts of Incorporation' of 1536 and 1542 made English the sole official language in Wales and also funded a network of courts and bureaucracy – in effect an English Language Act. The Education Act of 1870 made English the sole language of instruction in Wales, and by doing so created a new market for the English language press among the Welsh working classes. The British state might have taken the same road as the Hapsburg Empire, which decreed in its education act of 1867 that the medium of instruction in primary schools would be in the pupils' mother tongue, and by doing so created a viable market for languages like Slovene and Czech.

The Education Act of 1870 was supported by a massive investment of capital in the building of hundreds of new schools, training and paying thousands of new teachers, and publishing hundreds of thousands of textbooks. This on a scale which, if done in a Welsh language context, would be called 'nation-building' or even 'nationalist'. When one considers the financial commitment undertaken by the British state to turn Wales from a majority Welsh-speaking nation into a majority English-speaking one, the sums discussed today in similar debates in Wales are miniscule if not laughable.

The *Y Byd* project is also important for the health of a diverse news outlet in Wales – a news agenda which is controlled almost entirely by the BBC and Trinity Mirror, with chinks of light from magazines such as *Cambria*. It is also important from the point of view of creating a literate Welsh public.

The whole argument about funding of *Y Byd* has repercussions for the Welsh print media in English. A literate Welsh culture, in both languages, is imperative for the well being of Wales. Civic nationality goes hand in hand with literacy. An illiterate identity is a tribal identity. So, should not our whole political effort be to create a more literate nationality? Should not the Welsh state do all it can to make publishing in Wales easier? Thankfully, the Assembly Government has acted on this in varying degrees, but many would like to see a quantum change. Why not tax exemptions for Welsh publishers? Why does the Welsh state subsidise stupidity – drunks receiving treatment 'free at the point of delivery' for their own self-inflicted injuries, or doctors prescribing shampoo as part of the famous free prescriptions policy – but seem more circumspect about 'subsidising' literacy? For instance, just 0.5 per cent of the Assembly's health budget amounts to some £40m, or almost a quarter of the current budget of the Heritage Department.

The moral purpose of the Welsh state is to promote the Welsh language and Welsh culture through the medium of Welsh and English. That's its whole point. The morality of our state is to overturn centuries of discrimination against the indigenous language. Everything else can be done by another state.

If the British state is willing to send men to war to promote and defend the English language, then the Welsh state should be ready to do everything in its power to create a truly bilingual, literate Welsh nation. If it won't do that, then the vehicle for change that is the Welsh state, and the very concept of Wales, has lost its moral purpose.

If that's the case, then there is no point to Wales.

Cambria, volume 9, number 6, March-April 2008

Photography and Text

Visit our website for further information:
www.carreg-gwalch.com

Orders can be placed on our
On-line Shop

Heritage

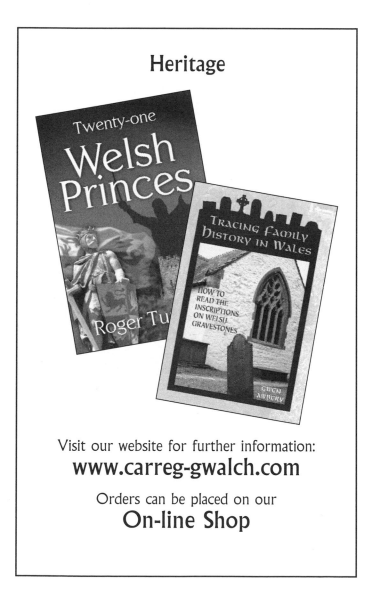

Visit our website for further information:
www.carreg-gwalch.com

Orders can be placed on our
On-line Shop

Biographies

Visit our website for further information:
www.carreg-gwalch.com

Orders can be placed on our
On-line Shop